D1572202

"This very *honest* book reflects well the views of those of us in Latin America who work with visiting teams. What a difference it would make if everyone believed (as these authors do) that the primary purpose of short-term missions is to foster relationships between brothers and sisters for the sake of a truly global church! This book casts a vision for a new way forward that is more contextually relevant, effective, and dignifying."

—MIZRAIM TOVAR AND KARLA MENDOZA
El Centro Liderazgo, Honduras

"Once upon a time, a small American church decided that rather than spend thousands of dollars sending a team overseas, they would ask a young man from Africa to travel to them so they could help him get education . . . When he returned to Burkina, he started a Christian school and a medical clinic. That young man was me—and I stand with these authors when they contend that with imagination and courage, we can discover better ways to love and serve the world."

—CALEB TINDANO
Clinique Médicale Shalom, Burkina Faso

"From my experiences hosting short-term teams in Thailand, I can affirm the message of many of the authors in this book: if foreigners want to be part of impactful work that is sustainable for the long term, they must form *authentic relationships* with the local people and *work alongside them* as coequals. This book helps us to understand why this must become the new normal for short-term missions and shows us where to begin."

—SUPUNNEE PARGUL
Program Director, Shared Space for All, Thailand

"This book is a tremendous achievement. For decades, short-term missions have had a noteworthy impact on communities and ministry organizations around the world. Sometimes with great value and sometimes with disastrous outcomes, but usually somewhere in between. This work pulls together diverse voices with well-informed perspectives . . . It will undoubtedly shape the vision and practice of STM for years to come! It is a must-read for anyone involved in overseas ministry."

—MYAL GREENE
CEO, World Relief

"Finally! A book that helpfully addresses the troublesome and critically important questions that surround short-term service projects. This is a must-read for anyone considering organizing a project. The diverse authors each bring vital insights. Not just an anti-STM, anti-neocolonialism rant, it provides pivotal insights for how to approach STM in ways by which everyone will benefit and the gospel of God's grace will be honored."

—TIM DEARBORN
Author of *Short-Term Missions Preparation Workbook*

"I have a love-hate relationship with short-term mission trips that too often are more about collecting Instagram fodder than anything related to the kingdom of God. These essays offer insightful ways forward to something more beautiful—even while unapologetically naming the things that undermine the ways of Jesus. Here are some practical pathways to follow and practiced theological perspectives from a *global* community of voices that can help us reimagine the future."

—RUTH HUBBARD
Director, Urbana Student Missions Conference

"Anything worth doing is worth doing well. Short-term missions have become a major part of local church ministry for years, but often with little evaluation and too little regard for those hosting them. This book offers helpful and hopeful content that not only recognizes key issues with STMs but also gives a litany of helpful counsel for future trips. This is a must-read book for anyone involved in the leadership of STMs."

—ED STETZER
Dean of the School of Mission, Ministry, and
Leadership, Wheaton College

"As a Turkish national who has hosted short-term teams in Istanbul, I highly welcome and recommend this honest book. These essays explain some of the common mistakes that are made, but also provide balanced, seasoned wisdom for nurturing collaboration and mutual learning. I am certain that this book will be a blessing for all who want more holistic understanding that can only lead to better approaches to STM."

—ENGIN YILDIRIM
Church of England

"This book urges us to enter into short-term missions with a willingness to learn and defer. As a Black man, I resonate with this admonition, since I've often interacted with people who have presumed that they knew more about my communities than I did—even though they did not live with or look like the residents. While this book doesn't attempt to address all of the problems with STM, I'm ordering it for all my staff!"

—JIMMY MCGEE III
CEO/President, The Impact Movement

"Burns and Inslee packed a lot of wisdom into this book. As a trained missiologist, I urge you: don't plan another trip until you and your team have studied this book together. It will make a world of difference for everyone involved."

—RANDY WOODLEY
Author of *Decolonizing Evangelicalism*

"The authors of this book not only explore the present status of STMs in a clear-eyed fashion but offer important 'maps' for developing new systems that will make the church stronger and more able to truly live as Christ followers in the present world. A must-read for Christian leaders from both sides of the economic and political divide!"

—RANDALL BORMAN
Executive Director, Cofan Survival Fund, Ecuador

Re-Imagining Short-Term Missions

Re-Imagining Short-Term Missions

Edited by
FORREST INSLEE
and ANGEL BURNS

Foreword by
Miriam Adeney

WIPF & STOCK · Eugene, Oregon

RE-IMAGINING SHORT-TERM MISSIONS

Wipf & Stock
An Imprint of Wipf and Stock Publishers
199 W. 8th Ave., Suite 3
Eugene, OR 97401

www.wipfandstock.com

PAPERBACK ISBN: 978-1-6667-1291-9
HARDCOVER ISBN: 978-1-6667-1292-6
EBOOK ISBN: 978-1-6667-1293-3

03/07/22

To my grandparents, Walter and Pauline Routh.
Thank you for living a life of saying "yes" to the Lord.

And to my husband Trevor—
My greatest support and love of my life.

Angel

To all who were once my students—
cultivating community, advocating for justice, and practicing mercy
in places all across the globe:
I'm grateful for all you've taught me.

Forrest

Contents

Foreword

The Migration of the Wildebeests

MIRIAM ADENEY

IF PASTORS KNOW ONLY one thing about missions, they must know how to run short-term projects. That is what the church expects. That's the bottom line.

In an ideal world, or in another era, this might not be a priority. In our time, however, short-term efforts are a dominant mission activity. Our challenge then, is to redeem and transform them into valuable, beautiful, significant activities. That is why this book is so important.

Missions is the heartbeat of Christian living. God is not just ours. Jesus is not our private Savior. God loves everybody, all the peoples, and especially the vulnerable, those who have been marginalized spiritually and materially. Missions—sharing God's love across boundaries—must be a major focus for healthy Christians. It should shape how we handle our time, money, and preoccupations.

A natural channel for this concern seems to be short-term missions. But there are significant problems. These problems must be addressed because they are not trivial. In fact, like bad medicine, bad engineering, or bad cooking, bad mission practice can hurt people. We can damage people through STMs (short-term missions).

This book nails some of the problems—and explores elements of solutions. For example, we must take time to show serious respect to the people on the ground, however inconvenient that is (and however difficult when another language is involved). If we truly believe all people are equal, we must stop and listen to them. We must ask ourselves: Do we seek and follow the counsel of thoughtful and appropriately skilled indigenous people *before* planning our short-term projects? Does our work empower locals, leaving them with greater confidence to apply their own resources to solve their problems? Are we determined to be part of long-term systemic solutions, rather than piecemeal efforts? If not, then what must we change, and what must we stop doing?

This re-oriented approach to mission is enormously less efficient than planning a project in our own country and then heading out to implement it. This takes time. It is not mastered in the first week off the plane. Yet we remember that God in Jesus spent thirty-three years in one place. Ultimately, our short-term work must fit in with and be subordinate to what long-term people are doing.

"We benefited so much!" short-term teams may report. But should that be top priority? Mission is not therapy. Christ did not come primarily to enhance his own experience. Nor do we do mission to enhance ours. Neither is a mission project's goal mainly to stimulate church giving or teambuilding. Instead, mission is meant to serve the recipients. And so, we can ask in all honesty, how do our field partners evaluate the results of these trips?[1]

I once heard a Kenyan pastor, looking over the annual influx of short-term teams passing through Nairobi, say, "They're like the colorful migrations of the wildebeests and zebras, each group in their own matching T-shirts." His observation prompts us to ask: Are vast numbers of minimally-trained short-term teams roaming the globe the best use of mission money, and the best way to serve genuinely needy people? Or can we do better?

Of course we can. There are positive strategies that can be followed to improve our STMs, and this book outlines some. On the material level, for example, we can buy supplies locally. While this might be the more difficult or less efficient choice, it is usually the better choice, because it strengthens the local economy and affirms the use of indigenous materials and networks.

We can train our team members to be well-rounded agents of blessing—helping them to absorb our destination communities' contexts and

---

1. To discover this, chapter 8, by Gena Thomas includes a helpful partnership analysis set of twenty questions, 94–104.

priorities (and even some of their language), but also immersing them in knowledge of Scripture, spiritual disciplines, culture knowledge, local church history, and interpersonal skills. Even if the witness of a team is intended mostly to be one of "Christian presence"—and not overt evangelistic activities—team members should all be able to give an answer for the hope that is in them. Teams that are well-prepared to offer clear, compelling, contextual witness can do so in the most formidable places; poorly prepared teams let the chances of a lifetime slip through their fingers.

Meanwhile, God is not asleep before we arrive on the scene. God is active everywhere. In many places there are not only local believers but also a body of Americans, Koreans, Brazilians, Filipinos, Germans, British and others onsite who speak the language, live much like the locals, and worship and lead shoulder to shoulder with those believers. While we need to watch out for the "expatriate lifestyle," our short-term teams can also plug into this multicultural community in order to minimize any potential problems.

This collection of essays calls attention to important aspects of short-term missions like these—and exhorts us to re-imagine better ways forward. In their contribution to this volume, Kennedy, Onyango, and Cook sum it up well:

> Compassionate Westerners who want to make a difference in any area of need in the world would do well to practice more mutuality and respect in intercultural partnerships, and more imaginative, context-informed approaches to addressing actual needs as defined by those who live in the context. Only then might they learn to stand alongside their brothers and sisters in other nations and understand themselves as coequal members of the wider global church whose purpose it is to enact God's love and mercy for the whole world.[2]

The practitioners and scholars whose voices are represented here challenge all of us to practice the courage and creativity required to make something beautiful out of the broken elements of short-term mission practices.

Miriam Adeney

As Associate Professor of World Christian Studies, Miriam Adeney teaches anthropology in the School of Theology at Seattle Pacific University. Her books include *Kingdom Without Borders: The Untold Story of Global*

2 See Kennedy, Onyango, and Cook's observations in chapter 7 of this volume, 79–93.

Christianity; *Daughters of Islam: Building Bridges with Muslim Women*; *God's Foreign Policy: Practical Ways to Help the World's Poor*; *Refugee Diaspora (with Sam George)* and others. Elected to the presidency of the American Society of Missiology, Miriam also has served extensively on the World Evangelical Alliance Mission Commission, the Lausanne Movement Diaspora Task Force, and the board of *Christianity Today*. She has received a Lifetime Achievement Award from Christians for Biblical Equality, and a Lifetime Training Award from Media Associates International. Miriam speaks at conferences and delivers distinguished lectures and teaches modular courses on six continents and at many North American locations. She holds a Ph.D. in anthropology from Washington State University, a M.A. in journalism from Syracuse University, and a B.A. in anthropology from Wheaton College.

Preface

FORREST INSLEE

THIS BOOK, AND MOST of the essays in it, were conceived before the CO-VID pandemic united the world in common suffering. The original intent of the collection was to encourage a broad re-thinking of the practices surrounding short-term missions. So when global travel was brought to a standstill—and short-term missions trips put on indefinite hiatus—we wondered if there was any point to putting out a book about something that was no longer happening!

What we soon realized, however, is that this is in fact exactly the right time for a re-evaluation of short-term missions. What else besides a global catastrophe could stymie all our plans and shut down intercontinental travel, giving us a perfect opportunity to take an honest look at the way short-term missions has been done? Given that it will be some time still before global travel fully resumes to a pre-pandemic pace, there is still time to pause, reevaluate, and ask ourselves:

- *What have we been doing in the name of short-term missions?*
- *And what ought we to be doing in the future?*

This is a book that is intended to help you and your community answer these critical questions.

If you picked up this book, chances are you already believe that the practices of short-term missions are in need of serious reform. Even before the pandemic, there had been a growing energy for a broad rethinking of the STM industry. Many are calling for increased creativity, contextuality, and mutuality. As the criticism regarding STMs becomes more accepted, there are courageous practitioners who have not lost hope, but instead have begun experimenting with new approaches that challenge the status quo and offer new ways forward. This book is a platform for these visionaries who are calling for better ways for the church to engage the needs of the world. By sharing their experiences, our hope is to foster a dynamic of critical rethinking and creative re-imagination about the ways that the *global* body of believers might interact and collaborate on a new basis.

Whatever your connection to short-term missions then, it is our hope that you will find in this book ideas that both challenge and encourage. The authors represented here write for those who are dismayed by the failures of present STM practices; we write too for those who desire to advocate for change but may not know what change looks like. This is a book for discontented missions pastors and youth group leaders who feel compelled to do something in the realm of formational cross-cultural missions, yet don't want to employ the same tired models that they know are ineffective at best. We write to equip Christian college missions and voluntourism coordinators who wish to meet the formational needs of their clients, but who seek ways that minimize cultural disruption and harm. We write to encourage approaches that foment processes of personal transformation, disabuse would-be mission travelers of false narratives of cultural and economic superiority, and equip people for humble, informed, responsible global citizenship. Importantly, we also write to give hope to those on the receiving end of STMs—the representatives of host cultures who long to see a better investment of resources, to see their people less disrupted and dishonored by current STM praxis, and who dream of a more collaborative, co-creative, coequal relationship to partner churches in various parts of the world.

It is our contention then that it is time for truth-speaking in love. It is time to confront bad practice that oppresses and dishonors people and reinforces inequalities. We are all part of one church; we are all of equal worth in God's eyes; we need one another's differences in order to think and act rightly. These are not the ideas that most short-term mission activities reflect today, and the global church needs to consider alternative voices. The authors of this book offer this sort of bold critique and suggest creative possibilities that inspire both sending and receiving communities to seek a higher standard when seeking to live out God's call to mission.

Introduction

Angel Burns and Forrest Inslee

This is a time of great change in short-term missions. The models that have become dominant in the past few decades—along with the sometimes-problematic assumptions that inform them—are being called into question. Not only are most short-term mission (STM) efforts being exposed as ineffective—they are also being shown to cause damage to those they are meant to help. As a result, calls for a more collaborative, just, and thoughtful STM ethos are being sounded through missions-focused conferences, books, journals, and social media. Increasingly (and very importantly) a mounting number of those voices are advocating for reformation from places conventionally referred to as "host" contexts. And yet, while new ideas about re-imagining short-term missions are emerging, far too many practitioners—in churches and other "sending" organizations—remain detached from, and often unaware of, this shift in the global conversation. *This must change.* Real, practical, systemic transformation will happen only when STM practitioners at the *grassroots level*—both senders and hosts—have the courage to design entirely new approaches that fundamentally challenge the status quo. This book is a call to action for such reformers . . .

and a challenge to those who love the church enough to devote themselves to what must become a revolution in short-term missions.

Our goal in this book is in part to examine current STM practices through a critical, evaluative lens. While STMs were born out of good intentions, certain biases and assumptions about culture and mission have shaped them into often harmful experiences for those hosting *and* for those being sent. Yet, while this book does offer critical insight, it is important to note that it is not *primarily* a critique of short-term mission trips. Those books have already been written. While the problematic nature of STM is assumed by our contributors, it is only a starting point—and that is because the authors in this book are convinced and compelled by the challenge of re-imagining *what short-term missions must become*. We refuse to turn a blind eye to the harm that STMs cause; at the same time, we refuse to give up hope that there are better ways for churches from all cultures and contexts—the global church—to work together to achieve God's missional purposes.

The authors in this book use "short-term mission," or STM, because it is the term that is commonly used to describe the various forms of service or learning-based travel practiced today. Nevertheless, we argue that it is a problematic term that needs to be critically evaluated, and even replaced with other more nuanced, more accurate descriptors. The use of the term "mission", for example, assumes that those being "sent" are the first to bring the good news of the gospel to a new place. That is rarely true of STM trips, and more often groups are sent out to visit and assist existing organizations or churches (which is arguably the healthiest way to practice short-term trips—but why call it "mission"?). Many of this book's authors also reject the notion that "mission"—the call of God to his people to bring the love of Jesus to all—can even be accomplished in a short-term timeframe without becoming objectifying and essentially transactional (as is sadly the case with so many short-term trips). Many of the practitioner-authors in this book believe that renaming STMs is essential groundwork for the larger project of re-imagination that must take place.

Readers will come to this book from a diversity of perspectives. For many people, short-term mission trips have yielded good, even transformative experiences (both of the book's editors, for example, found their way into long-term mission commitments through short-term mission experiences). There are also many who believe that, in general, all STM activity must produce positive outcomes simply because they are initiated with good intentions. Of such readers, we simply ask that you consider these essays with an open heart, and with humility to hear the sometimes-difficult truths about the downsides of current STM practices.

On the other hand, if you are someone who already has a good sense of the financial waste, the shallow theology, and the unjust power dynamics that typify much of STM praxis, we would urge you as well to read with humility and openness to the perspectives of those who still have hope for a reformed approach to STM. Many contributors to this book seek to re-imagine *new and better ways* for churches to engage the needs of the world, and offer some element of vision for a new way forward.

While some of the authors here suggest critical adaptations of existing STM models, others call for approaches that are so radically different that it is better to understand them as displacements or replacements of the old STM paradigm altogether. In the spirit of disruptive creativity then, our contributors offer a diversity of views that complement and sometimes contradict one another. Such is the nature of innovative conversation: fundamental change will happen only when we find the courage to speak alternatives—to give voice to new ways of thinking and doing that challenge the status quo, resist the power dynamics that keep us locked into unhelpful practices, and confront the idols of tradition and false orthodoxy.

Shifting the Paradigm

The essays in this volume are oriented around two core, interrelated themes that, taken together, help us to imagine a paradigm shift in short-term mission praxis:

- *Copowerment:* At the heart of this new paradigm is the value we call *copowerment.* "Copowerment" is a word that stands in contrast to the implied power differential of the word "empowerment"; we define it as *a dynamic of mutual exchange through which both sides of a social equation are made stronger and more effective by the other.* Of course, this dynamic requires an essential stance of humility for all involved—as well as authentic, non-voyeuristic curiosity and teachability.

- *Global church:* When our authors write about the *global church,* what they mean is quite simple. It is a purposefully broad term because it is meant to acknowledge that *Christians exist in nearly every part of the world.* In this book, we encourage readers to *act* as part of the global church, which simply means acknowledging that we are part of this larger body and must support and learn from one another. The authors in this book make the case for understanding "sending" and "host" churches as *coequal, collaborative participants in the broader community of global churches*. In keeping with this global church ethos, it is important to note that a good number of essays in this collection are written by representatives of host communities.

Copowerment: Trusting Ourselves to the Strengths of Others

My (Forrest) passion for rethinking STMs has to do with the fact that my life has been profoundly influenced by experiences of STM that were done well. I served as a full-time missionary in Istanbul for a number of years, and out of that experience founded a graduate program focused on effective cross-cultural service. Those vocational choices grew out of a short-term trip I took with my church when I was in my late twenties.

That STM to Istanbul occurred because we had been invited by a small group of young Turks who had recently chosen to become Christ-followers. We spent a lot of time with our Turkish hosts, sharing meals and stories, and getting to know one another. One man, who became a close friend and ministry partner, asked if I would return to help them start a church. Thus began a long-term partnership between Christ-followers in two very different contexts; several years (and multiple short-term trips) later, I did return to help them start what was by then their *second* church.

Importantly, my *sending* churches in the U.S. supported me on the condition that my work in Istanbul would be entirely directed and overseen by Turkish leadership. This allowed me the freedom from the baggage of a foreign agenda, and allowed me to better approach my work from a stance of receptivity and teachability; it also allowed my Turkish coworkers to decide the most effective ways for me to serve. On the one hand, I entered the Turkish context with skill sets that weren't already represented in the community. Yet there was much more that I didn't know—about how my knowledge of social entrepreneurship, for example, would need to be adapted to the realities of Turkish culture. And I had no idea what sorts of business endeavors made sense in light of local resources or community needs. I could have chosen to ignore my knowledge deficits, and to "empower" those I came to serve with what I had to offer in the typically top-down power dynamic of foreign experts. Instead, I entered into a very different, essentially coequal, fundamentally relational mode that my Turkish friends offered: I learned to empower others with the skills and resources that I could offer, *but also to be empowered in turn* with the inherent strengths, contextual resources, and local knowledge of my Turkish colleagues. In other words, we entered into a relationship of mutual empowerment—or *copowerment* as we refer to in this book.

The experience of that dynamic of copowerment has profoundly shaped all of my subsequent cross-cultural service and teaching to this day. As I worked alongside my Turkish ministry partners, trusting myself to their strengths as they trusted themselves to mine, I came to believe that the future of missions must be re-imagined in ways that bring churches throughout the world into collaborative ministry on a co-equal basis. I am convinced that we can reframe short-term mission as an essentially co-created endeavor—and as an opportunity to remake STM practices so that all parts of the global church can work together to innovate new STM practices that bring mutual blessing.

The *Global* Church: Redefining the Objectives of Short-term Missions

The assumption that any new approach to STM must be re-imagined by and for the *global church*, is a core principle expressed throughout this book. For me (Angel) the prospect of a more globally-collaborative approach to STM is what most motivates and excites me when thinking about short-term mission reformation. After living in Tokyo in 2015, I began leading STM trips. Back home in the States, as I spoke about these trips, I would tell stories of how the teams would exchange testimonies with church members, worship together, and minister alongside them. At some point, I would inevitably be asked: "But what did you *do* there?" Traditional STMs tend to miss out on the understanding that their beauty is often found in simply being *together*. This is the part of the STM experience that we need to hold onto. Short-term trips can reflect a piece of heaven on earth—God's kingdom come—when they share and celebrate diverse cultures, theology, understanding, identity, and worship. This is what my teams, along with Christ-followers in Japan, were "doing"—they were simply being the church. Not the American church, or the Baptist church, or the Western church—but *the* church in the world. Through new approaches to STM we can teach each other, hold each other, pray for one another, and move forward—bringing God's good news to this world *together.*

One phenomenon of the church's globalization is that congregations all over the world are mobilizing to send people out for short and long-term missionary endeavors. However, because the majority of STMs are still sent by the American church to the rest of the world, this book puts more emphasis on an honest but hopeful critique of American short-term mission practices. Another outcome of an increasingly interconnected global church is that those who are typically seen as hosts or receivers of short-term teams have been finding ways to offer both critique of and alternatives to conventional STM practices. We have included a good number of those voices in this book; they help make the case that the role of the host must be re-imagined so that healthy partnerships and authentic relationships become the norm in any new STM dynamic. At the heart of this book is the assumption that we, as churches in diverse cultural contexts, need one another to explore answers to such difficult questions. We are better together.

Motivating Values of STM Reformers

While there are many new, practical ideas represented in the chapters that follow, our aim in this book is not to offer new methods to replace the old. Instead, our hope is to inspire would-be STM reformers to innovate, and to work with their global church partners to design and experiment with radically new practices grounded in the specific opportunities, needs, and resources that each community brings to the table. This work of collaborative re-imagination though is not simply about creating new and better things to do in the name of short-term mission. Rather, the real work of STM reformation is *changing ourselves* as individuals and communities; we need to become the sort of people who will think and act differently. The STM revolution begins with us and with our communities. What the authors of this book offer then is inspiration to become the sort of people who have what it takes to do the work of collaborative re-imagination that will yield true, deep, systemic change.

So, while there are great ideas about different ways to do STM in this book, the more important impact will be the transformation of our very selves and our communities. We need to become the humble, courageous, inventive sort of people who are then able to design new models for intercultural exchange and service. To that end, we have brought together the perspectives of people who are already challenging the status quo by their actions. While their missional innovations are diverse and varied, these practitioners were invited to write for this book because they exemplify common characteristics of impactful STM reformers. Importantly, *they are qualities that should be sought by anyone who wants to be part of an STM reformation.* We've organized the book then around a framework of these prerequisite values:

- *Mutuality and Unity*
- *Humility and Repentance*
- *Curiosity and Teachability*
- *Creativity and Contextualization*

It is our hope that readers of this book will embrace these values as aspirational goals on the path to becoming agents of change in their own communities.

Engagement with the Text

This collection of essays invites active, authentic engagement. It is intended to encourage transformations of the heart and mind described above, and to equip individuals and communities for processes of deep re-imagination. In each section you'll find questions that invite you to pause and become more aware of your assumptions about STM practices. You'll also find prompts that challenge you to innovate new possibilities for learning and service-oriented travel, or to generate new collaborative models for intercultural, interchurch collaboration. This sort of dialogic engagement might not be comfortable for some; resisting cultural inertia and questioning deeply entrenched assumptions is never easy. Nevertheless, what the world needs now—what we *all* need now—is the courage to go beyond mere tweaks to the methodological status quo of short-term missions today. The writers of this book invite you to put aside old models and to participate with them in fostering creatively-disruptive, reformational change. We urge you to seek nothing less than the reformation of your own STM praxis—as individuals and as local communities—that will ultimately lead to transformation of *who we are together* as the global community of Christ-followers.

As you undertake the work of re-imagination, it is important to keep in mind that there is grace in the process of change—and that ultimately it is *God's* process of change. The sort of cultural, perspectival, worldview changes we aspire to—especially when it comes to changing our communities—may take more time than we want it to. At best we can resolve to make the changes we are able to make in the moment, and to seek courage for the changes we have yet to face when the right time comes.

As challenging as it is to work for a paradigm shift, it is our hope that you will experience the excitement that comes from the adventure of building something new—and the deep satisfaction that comes from being part of something much bigger than ourselves. We invite you to hope for new models that can reform or even replace less-effective modes of STM. Our prayer is that God will fill us with dreams of a new way of missional thinking-and-being that inspires innovative practices, and connects members of the global church in copowering, mutually transformative community.

SECTION ONE

Mutuality and Unity

A KEY ASSUMPTION THAT has shaped this essay collection is that STM reform can never result from a one-sided conversation: *any critical and regenerative conversation about short-term missions must involve a diversity of voices from churches all over the world.* This requires the hard work of building relationships on new foundations. When all who are involved in the STM dynamic are able to acknowledge and overcome the unhealthy relational dynamics of the past, they free themselves to encounter each other as coequal members of one global church. When they are able to *acknowledge their need of one another,* copowerment becomes possible.

Quite intentionally, we've included voices from host contexts—that is, those communities and organizations that tend to be on the receiving end of short-term visits. Richard Twiss, author of the book *One Church, Many Nations,* once said:

> In scripture, Paul uses the analogy of the human body to describe how people from different cultural and ethnic backgrounds can relate together as followers of Jesus. What he says is that every part is vitally important if the whole body is going to be healthy. Well, Native people are almost completely absent from places of influence in the western church because we've been relegated to "the mission field"—so we're not considered to have anything of value to contribute to the wider body of Christ, [yet the church needs to acknowledge]: "We are in desperate need of the contributions

3

of our Native brothers and sisters, so Lord helps us to humble ourselves so we can recognize what those contributions are, to make room in our own places as people in positions of power, and to hear the voice from the margins that would bring a corrective word from heaven."[1]

His words, of course, are true on a much broader scale when it comes to the American church's stance toward most other parts of the church in the world. By including a broader diversity of voices than is typically heard in the larger conversation about short-term missions, this book seeks to resist that stance, and to model a more honest—and frankly, more interesting—conversation that can generate profound innovations in STM praxis.

Mutuality and unity as guiding values for STM reformers, then, help us to recognize and resist power inequalities, and remind us to respect the unique gifts and capacities represented in collaborative intercultural relationship. Through mutuality, we share our cultures and celebrate the diversity of the world while ministering together in unity—thus all parts of the global church body can work together to innovate new responses to God's invitation to witness and proclamation. The next chapters exhibit these characteristics of mutuality and unity in unique ways, and provide examples of how these traits play out in STM reform.

1. Richard Twiss, personal interview.

1

Reframing Short-Term Trips through Authentic Relationships

Robert Katende *with* Lisa San Martin

The year was 2004. Two young people appeared in my village and said, "We are on a short-term mission trip from our church. Will you show us what you are doing?" "Of course," we said, welcoming them, "let us show you around!" They toured every part of our facilities, and took videos, claiming a desire to show their "friends" our work. Months later, we found that these videos were being used to raise money for a well-known and widely criticized nonprofit organization. We were shocked. We would never have supported such a deceptive use of images from our community.

While we do find that *most* STM participants are well-meaning, the dangers and complexities of such trips make them very easy to critique. In our context, while STMs under local guidance can be very helpful for evangelism, they are not the most *effective* tool for sustainable community development projects, or discipleship. Locals, and sometimes long-term missionaries, have the contextual understanding necessary for more sustainable results. And occasionally, as seen in the story above, STM can be a disaster.

With such an introduction, you might expect me to make a case in this essay that we should stop doing STM entirely. But that is not actually my position. In spite of the dangers, and the potential for ineffectiveness, I love STM—as long as certain parameters are observed. At the organization I founded—Som Chess Academy in Kampala, Uganda—we cultivate mutual relationships based on respect and learning, and develop true partnerships with those who are willing to adapt and break from the traditional roles associated with STM. We have come to believe that the most important element of STMs, or any other form of mission work today, is true relationship.

Reframing our Understanding of "Effective"

It's important to ask if STM trips are effective. However, we must *first* determine what we mean by the term "effective," because how we judge an STM or program can really depend on one's cultural lens. Visitors from western contexts are very often focused on efficiency, and on the best investment of resources (most often financial resources, as well as temporal). This approach usually entails targeting these resources toward specific projects. Many voices now question the effectiveness of STM by looking at their project efficiency. Of course, locals can often get projects done more efficiently (with certain exceptions—including some kinds of evangelism trips in my context). So from this perspective, on average, STMs really aren't very effective.

However, if we assume that all problems are related to resources, then we risk reducing missions to a financial puzzle comprised of two parts: evangelism and poverty relief. Conventional mission engagement is too often founded on the premise that poverty (and even church growth) is all about a lack of financial resources—*rather than a condition of broken relationships.* When this happens, those involved naturally defer to whoever has the most material resources to solve local problems.

The premise that poverty is merely a lack of financial resources is so commonly accepted in the West that many readers may be taken aback at the possibility of an alternative way of thinking. You may be wondering what I mean by "broken relationships." As Brian Fikkert and Kelly Kapic explain in *Becoming Whole,* true wealth consists of wellness in four relationships: with God, self, others, and creation.[1] In fact, this multifaceted relational wellness is the truest aim of missions. Evangelism and material poverty relief are not the striving twin goals of missions, between which the

---

1. Fikkert and Kapic, *Becoming Whole,* 165.

various denominations must choose. God's goal and hope for the world, and for all communities, is *shalom*: a deep wellness that applies to all the integrated parts of one's being and one's community. It includes spiritual, physical, emotional, and mental wellness . . . and it is, above all, relational in nature. Western "evangelical Gnosticism" separates the spirit from the body and thus pits physical wellbeing against spiritual wellbeing, as if the two aims were in competition—making even missions a personal and individualistic pursuit.[2] In contrast, holistic mission (also known as integral mission), unites these aims in a framework of relational wholeness which can only be discovered in community. This community mindset can be expanded to encompass our relationship as part of the global church and then, the global church can strive for shalom *together*.

Our culture in Uganda happens to be less individualistic than the cultures of most westerners, which gives us an advantage when pursuing *shalom*. I often hear this from visitors: "You have so little, but you are all so happy. I want to take this with me." They don't really mean that there is virtue in material poverty, but that they have begun to understand our relational wealth. Of course, using money wisely and completing projects is helpful too! But when relationships come first, it is possible to spend money in ways that may appear ineffective from a typical western, project-orientation perspective—but which are in fact very effective from a missional relationship perspective. In the mission partnerships surrounding Som Chess Academy, we have learned to speak about "effectiveness" in ways that keep relationships top of mind—and to teach our western partners to do the same. It is this alternative conception of effectiveness that allows us to focus our ministry on what we believe is truly important: people, relationships, and community.

From Projects to People: Copowerment

To travel even short distances here in Uganda can be very time-consuming, and that is only partly due to the terrible condition of some of the roads. When you tell a group of STM visitors that they are going to leave Kampala and go to another region, they will ask how many hours it will take to get there. What they don't understand is that, in Uganda, travel is never so straightforward. We drive, stop, take a break and chat, drive again, take a detour to check on a friend or relative, stop and chat with them for a

---

2. Fikkert and Kapic, *Becoming Whole*, 63.

time . . . and then before you know it, the six hours have become ten or more! This sometimes makes our western visitors impatient, and sometimes even angry. Thinking in terms of *efficiency* means hitting the road and pushing through to the destination. I have a certain way that I explain it to them: "You westerners have the watch, but we Ugandans have the time." This is not to say that we are intentionally careless about time; rather, in Uganda, it tends to come naturally to focus more on people than on tasks. And that takes time.

In Uganda, we are fortunate that our culture often helps us prioritize relational effectiveness over other kinds of effectiveness. But as noted above, we are all called to move toward a primary focus on effective relationships—which often means displacing a primary focus on effective projects. We must learn to slow down and see people as *people,* rather than as means to an end. If we are to work together on the basis of authentic relationship, we have to learn to ask questions of one another, to listen to each other, and to recognize our different (and complementary) strengths. Only when we take the time to cultivate mutual, interdependent connection can we truly *collaborate* in the best sense of that word; only then can we move forward together toward common practical goals.

Nowhere is this kind of intentional mutuality more critical—or more valuable—than in the collaborative work of the global church. There is no program or system for STMs that can guarantee copowerment dynamics on the ground. However, critical prior work includes the establishment of healthy relationships between individuals (and over time, between communities: churches, NGOs, etc.), so that future STMs can emerge—if appropriate—from the rich soil of those relationships. Before talk of STM, the original relationship—whether that is with an old friend, or an organizational leader, or an STM participant from a previous trip—must be given some time to grow, so that strong roots of understanding and commitment have time to develop. Only gradually can new people (who will require training and nurturing from both sides) be introduced into that established relationship—often via STMs. And these STMs do not necessarily have to be about projects! But the projects that are undertaken on this foundation of relationship and collaboration (whether directly involving the STM, or not) have a strong and sustainable impact. Interestingly, they also tend to be pretty effective in terms of resource investment and efficiency.

Through the years, we have watched STM visitors start great projects that were supposed to augment and support our ministry, but in the end proved to be more about their own (usually well-meaning) agendas. Sometimes in those cases, the short-term visitors did not follow through on their intentions to return; a few years down the road, the projects they started (and that were dependent on their support) fell apart. After a number of such disappointments, we eventually realized that their short-term focus was on the accomplishment of their projects, not on their relationships to us as a community. Projects *can't* be accomplished in a one-shot trip; they require ongoing relationships. We often have to say no to projects. Some people say, "I have resources, I wish I could do something outstanding." But resources alone won't accomplish anything. The real work begins with our friends who have ears to hear when we tell them: *no one can do anything outstanding here without a basis of real relationship.* And then these friends keep in touch: they write, they call, they hear about our visions, they ask questions, they answer needs, they organize connections . . . and then they return. That's when the real projects, the real possibilities, begin to come out and introduce themselves to us all.

We have thus become more confident to insist on a relational foundation with our foreign partner organizations: because we believe that this is what is required of the global church in an age of globalization. Since a relational orientation happens to be more ingrained in Ugandan culture, we deeply value our role in the global church modeling these priorities and discipling others to accept them. There are also project and efficiency benefits: a relational orientation does usually lead to better investment of resources in impactful, long-term sustainable programs. However, that's not the central reason we focus on relationships. Relationships are intrinsically important in a way that no project can be. They are sacred. In fact, we must even be careful to avoid approaching relationships as the first box to check on the project/efficiency plan. Many STM teams come to Uganda thinking *"What can I do to better these people?"* Relationships are not the first step to finding the answer to that question. Rather, if the relationships are healthy, the question will take a different, more mutual, form. The question as phrased is problematic: an indication that one is starting from a western project/efficiency mindset, and that the copowering elements of the relationship need strengthening. Of course, it is asked in innocence and with love, and it may be answered with grace. But it does not show that "these people" are truly seen. And it does not show an understanding of this important truth: that in a community development equation, each party has something to bring to the table. Unfortunately, some people think that they know it all—and the traditional mission framework has not done much to counter this naïve assumption. If STM visitors don't learn to really *see* those who are different from themselves, then they will be unable to surrender themselves to the strengths and insights of others—who in most cases actually have better solutions to their own community's problems.

The Danger of Exploitation

As the story I told at the start of this essay illustrates, one particularly damaging agenda that short-termers can fall into is one that emphasizes fundraising over authentic relationship. When motivating people back home to donate money becomes the primary goal—even if the cause is good and just—it inevitably leads to the objectification of people. In the worst examples of the fundraising focus, I have even seen some missionaries deliberately fail to address the critical needs of a community in order to create a scenario that would elicit sympathy from others and motivate them to give more money. Sadly, the fund-development approaches employed by NGOs and churches today too often depend on appealing to emotions. My heart aches when I see "commiseration" images on community development organizations' websites; what is sadder still is the fact that these images actually work! Unfortunately, the real story behind many of these photographs is one of inauthentic relationships with locals. Of course, missionaries and community development workers do not always realize it when they are exploiting people in their quest to "better" them. Nevertheless, if fundraising depends on the sharing of images and stories that emphasize only the negative aspects of a developing world context—and if a particular place and people are portrayed as essentially deficient and needy—then something is far off balance in that relationship. And if a missionary or organization capable of meeting a need decides instead to share images and postpone meeting the critical need, to raise more funds—that, friends, is exploitation, and antithetical to authentic relationship.

It is important to note that those who host short-term teams can also act exploitatively, and fail to see the missionaries as real people; we might instead view them through a lens of the influence they might represent—or out of our insecurities impose on them the role of "expert" or "judge." It is common for host communities, for example, to want to "dress up" the story of their work. When we were preparing to film *Queen of Katwe*, one of the film's directors-to-be came to Uganda to check on our story and our projects.

She had some doubts, knowing that ministries often exaggerate their work, and wanted to see how our ministry operated on a normal, day-to-day basis. She paid a surprise visit just as I was leaving to go on a trip of my own, so I left it to one of our young leaders to show her around. In the end she was happy with what she saw, but was especially impressed that I had not insisted on being there to filter the experience. It has become my practice, whether I'm there or not, to encourage any staff person or client of our ministry to freely interact with visitors and missionaries, and to share their own stories and stories of our work. This practice of "nothing to hide" continually reminds us that our mission does not exist for the sake of good impressions, or fundraising, or flashy projects. We exist for people, so we have to serve them with integrity. That also means that we respect our foreign short-term visitors enough to engage them as coequals, and to love them as sisters and brothers in the extended family that is the global church.

Friendship as the Shield against Exploitation

Good relationships between partners in missions—churches, organizations, and local communities—are not just about sending and receiving people. If we are willing to do the work, they can really be about friendship. Friends are interested in each other's lives, not just agreed-upon outcomes. They listen to each other's stories, and they help each other learn about one another; in so doing, they also learn about themselves. They warn each other when they sense potential risks and are honest to graciously point out one another's blind spots. Such copowered friendships really are the best inoculation against the more exploitative, transactional forms of interaction that are common in the realm of STM.

You may be wondering: isn't this view a bit extreme? Don't we all have transactional relationships in our lives? Of course. But these transactional relationships serve us better in low-risk situations, not high. For example, you might open a bank account without having a friend who works at the branch. However, I hope you wouldn't open a *shared* bank account with someone you didn't know well in real life (especially if it's a wealthy foreign widow who has emailed you about a once in a lifetime investment opportunity)! Likewise, we must take the time to build trust with potential ministry partners.

As globalization expands, the risk of exploitation becomes more intense—and true friendships become more valuable. In developing contexts, globalization is often thought of only in terms of large corporations attempting to exploit poor communities for resources like water and oil. However, "exploitation" happens whenever one party *uses* another to achieve a goal (no matter how worthy the goal may be). On more than one occasion, a respectable development organization has asked me to attest to the receipt of a much larger amount of funds than was actually donated to our ministry. When I refused, they put it firmly but diplomatically: "If I were you, I would refrain from stating the actual amount." Stories like these remind us of the importance of knowing those we work with well, and investing the time and energy it takes to develop trusting friendships.

It is unfortunate that globalization can make materially poor communities vulnerable to exploitation. However, globalization can also create opportunities to connect with international friends. For example, donor entities increasingly want to work directly with us these days, and global networks of communication and commerce make it possible to do so. In our context, these true friends are the ones who come to show us how to share our talents on a global scale rather than find ways to own or sell our resources for their own profit. So, we need such good, trustworthy friendships for collaborative opportunities, but also for protection against those who seek to exploit.

International friends like these in fact were instrumental in telling the story of Phiona and our chess-centered ministry; they helped us tell our story through a book, and that eventually became a Disney movie, and eventually people all over the world were inspired by the work we do. Our international friends have helped us to channel that notoriety in ways that support even more community development work in Uganda, and also in other countries. Eventually, the movie helped open doors which led me to a graduate degree. Even while I was earning my master's degree in development, I needed friends to help out in several ways, including encouragement, consultancy, editing, and participating in the interviews that were part of my studies. Of course, friends can't be treated only as resources or means to our own ends. Genuine friends are those who commit to a long-term, life-changing relationship that looks beyond project accomplishment. I cannot overstate the joy and comfort I take in my friendships with people around the world who genuinely care about me and about our work. In the most difficult times, the knowledge that they stand with me is incredibly sustaining. From experience I can say with my whole heart: we need international friends. We need each other.

The Results of Friendships Formed through Copowerment

When it comes to growing and expanding our international relationships, I have yet to find any realistic substitute for STMs. Yet in that framework, building copowering relationships beyond the functions of "sender" and "receiver" involves mentorship, discipleship, teaching, and training. There is a lot involved! We try to provide all four of these elements to those who come to visit us in Uganda, and we expect to be similarly influenced by those who come.

One story that illustrates this copowering dynamic is about a short-term participant who, as a result of her time with us, is now doing wonderful work in Lynchburg, Virginia. She was profoundly shaped by engaging in the work we do here, and formed a deep connection to us. In fact, she became so involved that when she got married, she even brought her new husband to Uganda for their honeymoon—and stayed for three months! We trained and mentored them in the processes and values of the work we do, and in the process became friends. In the end, both she and her husband were confident to say, "I think I can do this at home!" They returned to Lynchburg to start Crane's Ministry (named after our Ugandan national bird), and are now reaching out to children through sports as we do, yet in their own context. Such stories are not unusual.

Our relationship with the United States-based Sports Outreach Institute also expresses our value of mutual formation. The organization has been supporting our sports ministry over many years; rather than insist on building their own projects in Uganda, they work with us to support our ministry here on the ground. Through the course of our relationship, and through the sending of teams, they too learned from the strengths of our program even as they were sharing their teaching and resources with us. We eventually helped them launch ministries in the United States that draw from our model, and they have since expanded to many cities, taking what they learned (and continue to learn) to reach out to whole communities, and to children and the elderly in particular. And it's all because they chose to engage with us on the mutual basis of friendship, and allowed themselves to be formed by their experiences in what is often called the "mission field."

The Role of Host Redefined

When we have a right perspective of one another, we can begin to practice copowering relationships and reframe expectations on both sides of the missionary equation. And that begins with the belief that we are members of one family in God, and partners in the mission of the global church. Though I use the terms, I'm not sure that "sender" (or visitor) and "receiver" (or host) are very helpful in describing this dynamic. No matter who is traveling or to where, both parties ought to be sending and receiving in some form, and both sides should be experiencing change from the process.

It's natural and typical for STM leaders today to rely on their hosts for information and support. But if we reframe "effectiveness" primarily in relationship terms, then the role of the hosts as knowledgeable, mentoring educators takes on much greater significance. While relational poverty affects all cultures in different ways, in Uganda we find that we have relational wholeness paradigms to model and teach which are hard to find in the west. We have come to understand our role as "relational educators" to be part of our specific calling within the body of Christ. We really do consider it a calling and privilege to share our "wealth" of experiential, culture-based understanding with our brothers and sisters from abroad—just as we also, undeniably and with joy—receive so much from them. When I hear westerners evaluate STMs only in terms of whether they are an effective way for *them* to help *us*, I think they may be misinterpreting the value of our role as educators.

Everyone knows that many trip participants have their lives changed on mission trips. Yet many still wonder if that isn't, on some level, "using" or taking advantage of the people in developing countries who need to put effort into mentoring them while they are here. It's an excellent question that is consistent with a more respectful, relational orientation. However, I can say that those in my community in Uganda are *more* blessed when we give than when we receive. If anyone would partner with us, they must allow us to give too. We view our interactions with guests as valuable contributions to the work of the kingdom of God in fighting poverty (in all its forms), and opportunities to help establish flourishing communities of *shalom*. To be frank, our work with short-term visitors and the western communities that send them, gives us opportunities to alleviate a poverty of soul that comes from overreliance on all things material, and a poverty of relationship characterized by the objectification of people as projects.

Host communities, especially in the developing world, also have some responsibility to cultivate a more copowering dynamic in the STM equation. It takes intentional work to embrace a different role—and they often need encouragement to see the value of it. The legacy of colonization has conditioned many cultures to think of themselves as receivers only. Relational poverty exists in many forms, and while it may be most obvious in western culture, we aren't immune from our own version of it. We can, for example, get comfortable in the dehumanizing habit of seeing our STM guests only in terms of the material benefits they represent. And when we let outsiders assume responsibility for addressing the needs and issues that belong to us, we risk falling into complacency that prevents us from embracing our callings within (and responsibilities to) the body of Christ. True friends, working together across cultures as members of one global church, can help each other to avoid such pitfalls.

In truth, the key practice for doing STMs well applies to both senders and receivers: *cultivate authentic, mutual relationships, and maintain them over time.* STM trips are valuable to the extent that they emerge from and contribute to healthy, copowering relationships—which can in turn yield impactful, sustainable ministry. In these mutual relationships where everyone has something to give and receive, we see the strengthening of the church as a whole, and the possibilities of transformation for both visitors and hosts. Copowerment opportunities are all around us—even in STMs—if we are committed to keeping relationships central. As we learn to see people well, and to truly value our relationships, STMs can be reframed in ways that help us to build coequal, collaborative community in the wider context of the global church.

Robert Katende

Katende is best known as mentor to Phiona Mutesi, seen in the 2017 Disney movie, *Queen of Katwe*. Robert worked as a consultant, helping with the chess scenes, and assisting David Oyelowo (who played Robert) to achieve character originality. Coming from a disadvantaged background, he lived in the slums of Nakulabye before he made it to Kyambogo University, where he secured a degree in civil engineering and a Computer Engineering Degree from Kampala University. Later, he switched careers to social work through Sports Outreach Ministry and obtained a master's degree in International Community Development from Northwest University in Kirkland, Washington. He is the founder of SOM Chess Academy and the Robert Katende Initiative.

Lisa San Martin

Originally from Seattle, Washington, Lisa San Martin has lived in British Columbia, Ukraine, and Argentina, for studies and service in missions-related capacities. She currently serves as the Director of Student Services for the MA in International Community Development program at Northwest University (a degree she also earned). She is passionate about helping the western church better hear and understand voices from developing contexts.

Bibliography

Fikkert, Brian, and Kelly Kapic. *Becoming Whole: Why the Opposite of Poverty Isn't the American Dream*. Chicago: Moody, 2019.

2

Working Side by Side
A Better Way Forward in Short-Term Missions

EMMANUEL KAREGYESA *and* TOM RAKABOPA,
with EMILY CARMINATI

IN 2008, I (EMMANUEL) took a missionary from Asia to deliver training to local pastors in the rural villages of Rwanda. I was serving as both the translator and program manager for the host church. During our introductions, the missionary asked the participating pastors to share about the needs and work they were already doing in their communities. There was an awkward silence in the room. Finally, a lead pastor for the community stood up and said,

> Emmanuel, we are uncomfortable to share with you our stories. When visitors from the outside come here, they ask for stories and take our pictures, but we never get to see them again. We often find miserable stories of our children, families, and communities on the internet, but we never see those people back. Please deliver your training, come back later in the future, and maybe then we will tell you our stories.

The missionary kept insisting on getting those stories despite the pastors's clear discomfort. Her well-intended insistence, born out of a desire to promote this community's needs and draw from an international audience of donors, quickly became disrespect toward the local people's rights and dignity.

At their best, STMs bear beautiful fruit: visiting teams both serve and learn from their host communities, and unity within diversity grows within the body of Christ. Visiting teams and host churches are mutually encouraged and strengthened. The host church experiences fresh life as they welcome and receive loving strangers. The gospel is shared. The ministry is expanded.

At their worst, however, STMs create cultural misunderstandings, interrupt the work of the local church and community, and provide opportunities for well-meaning sending churches to "help" in ways that damage the community. STMs conducted in the way that has become traditional—with financially well-resourced western churches sending teams to materially poor churches in Africa and elsewhere—easily become breeding grounds for paternalism, disrespect, and mutual disappointment.

In this chapter, we wish to explore in more detail some of the benefits and challenges of STMs that we have observed from our perspectives as a development practitioner (Emmanuel) and host church leader (Tom). The examples we provide come from our experiences at Central Baptist Church (CBC) in Harare, Zimbabwe, the Anglican Church of Rwanda Diocese of Kigali, Rwanda, and the P.E.A.C.E. Plan ministry in Rwanda, where we have hosted STMs (both individuals and groups) for many years. Our desire is to increase candor and courage, specifically among those considered "host" churches. In our experience, we have seen the limitations of the traditional "host" and "sender" labels and are excited to dive beyond the norm and into an honest conversation about broadening the responsibilities and assumptions each partner holds. Listed below are our ideas for a better way forward for short-term-missions-sending churches and hosts:

- A global church approach to supporting and strengthening each other as churches, with support and ministry flowing in all directions—not just from financially wealthy churches to the financially poor.

- A posture of humility and equality from both sending and hosting churches that enables listening, sharing of candid feedback, and the building of short-term projects that truly benefit the local community.

- Long-term partnerships between hosting and sending churches that provide space for real relationships and shared, sustainable transformation.

A Global Approach

At the heart of traditional STM work around the globe is a damaging mind-set regarding who needs to be served and who can do the serving. From our perspective, this mindset seems to stem from a focus on poverty and resources rather than on the simple question of *how we can serve*. If we remove finances from the equation, a new kind of STM emerges: churches begin simply asking questions such as, "How can we serve our neighbor church? What skills do we have to share? What different perspective might we offer that might help our neighbors grow deeper in their marriages, their faith, their community development?" When the focus is on encouraging through shared experiences or partnering to offer the unique giftings God has given each church congregation individually—and not on financial resources or poverty—every church becomes a potential sending church. No longer must STMs entail well-financed churches in the West sending teams to "poor" churches in the Global South; now, churches in the West as well as in Africa, Asia, and South America can partner together for mutual encouragement and spiritual enrichment, regardless of their resources or lack thereof. When such STMs bring the global church together into a network of diverse, meaningful, enriching relationships, Christian unity can thrive.

Here, an example may be useful: one of Central Baptist Church's global partners is Honey Ridge Baptist Church, based in Johannesburg, South Africa. Honey Ridge Baptist used to host STM teams from around the world, before they too felt compelled to send small teams out to encourage Zimbabwean churches significantly affected by socio-economic and political challenges at that time. The Missions Pastor at Honey Ridge, Harold Twine, explained that,

> Our church, though already outward looking and involved in STMs, was challenged to do more when an unknown church reached out to us and wanted to know how they could encourage us. We felt God's hand move through their trip. After being the recipient of that STM, we reexamined ourselves and asked the question, "who are we encouraging in the same manner?" That was partly how we started our missions of mercy into Zimbabwe.

Today, Honey Ridge Baptist sends STMs to Central Baptist Church and to other Zimbabwean partners regularly on what they call "missions of mercy." The focus of each trip varies depending on local needs and Honey Ridge's current abilities and interests; for example, sometimes they collect medical supplies and bring them to a church that is providing community medical care; at other times they may come to encourage and train the young women at our *Rafiki* (Swahili for "friend") Girls' Centre, which supports underprivileged girls who are unable to complete their education. Whichever partner they come to serve, their intentional visits have created genuine local friendships and collaborations. STMs like these have left us (hosting churches) strengthened and encouraged by the presence of a fresh unity within God's church.

Our church, Central Baptist, has now experienced its own call to send as well as receive. In 2010, when a massive earthquake brought devastation to Haiti, our church was moved by the level of human suffering involved. We took time to reflect on the words Pastor Twine had shared with us: "Who are we encouraging in the same manner?" We wanted to follow the example of the Macedonian church, about which Paul writes, "Now, brethren, we wish to make known to you the grace of God which has been given in the churches of Macedonia, that in a great ordeal of affliction their abundance of joy and their deep poverty overflowed in the wealth of their liberality."[1] Despite our own financial struggles, we nevertheless raised $2000 for a Haitian church we did not know for their relief work with affected community members. This encouraging process was also the genesis of a missions committee in our church, tasked with thinking critically about ways that we might, as a regular practice, bless other churches in the world through STMs. As we've continued to be blessed *and* look for ways to bless others in the church, we have recognized more than ever the need to cultivate an outward focus, and to remind ourselves often that we are part of a global church.

While our ability to raise funds for another church in need was thrilling to us, it is important to note again that finances are not the only reason to engage with other churches around the world. For example, the Anglican Church of Rwanda Diocese of Kigali, Rwanda has sent teams of men to Uganda to share with the men of a local church community there about what it means to be a man—at home, in the church, in the community, at work. In this case, the mission activity is simply men sharing their daily experiences with other men from a somewhat different cultural context, sharing examples of their daily practices, encouraging each other to build meaningful relationships, and coming alongside young men in the church who are struggling with their relationships at home or with a lack of stable

---

1. 2 Cor 8:1–2 (NASB).

employment or source of income. We have also hosted countless mission teams sent to us from diverse places—teams of men and women with life experience to share, business skills to teach, or simply moral and spiritual support to offer our community members. This form of peer learning can be incredibly rich and beneficial to both sending and hosting churches! And as "a prophet is not without honor except in his own town," we find that sometimes it just takes a group of outsiders or a pastor from another context in the pulpit for a Sunday to share encouragement or truth and have it hit home in a way that a local pastor's words never will.[2] STM work of this kind—freed from an emphasis on geographical location or on material resources but focused instead on how one community might encourage another—multiplies the impact of all churches involved, fulfilling the Great Commission and bringing churches across the globe more closely into the love of Christ.

Every church can be a sending church if they approach STMs in this way, but not every church is poised to send every kind of team. If our men in Rwanda need to be encouraged in their marriages, who will be better positioned to encourage them? An American mission team bringing with them an American view of marriage, or a team from a neighboring African nation with a closer cultural view of marriage to ours? A posture of humility and cultural sensitivity is absolutely necessary to prevent the paternalism, cultural clashes, and potential harm that may occur if a sending church assumes it has something to offer that another church "needs." That posture is what we will turn to in the following section.

A Posture of Humility and Equality

While many STMs are mutually beneficial to sending and host churches, there are instances when they create disunity and harm. These instances usually stem from attitudes embedded within the sending church culture that (unintentionally) result in a lack of equality between sending and hosting churches, or from a lack of candor and humble listening on one or both sides. Both sender and host can be at fault in this realm; both have work to do to build a relationship of mutuality, equality, and shared encouragement.

A few years ago, one of the teams visiting our ministry in Zimbabwe brought very expensive water filters for a community in need of clean water. The need for clean water was real, but the affordable and sustainable

2. Mark 6:4 (NIV).

solution was not expensive water filters from another country that had to be replaced every twelve months! The money spent on buying and replacing those filters could easily have been spent instead on sinking a borehole and providing the whole community with a clean, accessible, and sustainable water source. Had the short-term team consulted, listened, and acted on local information and knowledge, an actual solution to the clean water problem might now be in place.

At the core of a situation like this one is a well-intended paternalistic posture assumed by many western sending churches. Instead of approaching the Zimbabwean church as an equal and peer—and assuming the presence of local knowledge, local innovations, and ongoing initiatives—the church who brought us the unsustainable water filters presumed to know what was best for a community on the other side of the world without actually asking. Sadly, they therefore missed out on the opportunity to make a lasting impact. While there often is some value in a foreign team's "out of the box" perspectives, personal experiences, and new ideas, these churches need to *start* by asking about and listening to their hosts real needs. They would do well to begin with the assumption that there are likely to be context-relevant, homegrown solutions for meeting those needs, and to look for ways to support them.

Jeff Rutt, the founder of HOPE International, tells a story of how an honest discussion with Pastor Petrenko from Zaporozhye in Ukraine revealed that Jeff's mission team and church were hurting the people and the very economy they had hoped to help. Jeff and his church had been shipping containers of food, clothing, and other supplies to this church for many years. During one short-term trip, the local pastor shared his profound thanks with Jeff and his team for their support of his church and community. But Pastor Petrenko also asked, "Is there not a way you can help us help ourselves?"[3] We encourage sending churches to set aside their assumptions, no matter how thoughtful and generous they are, about the "help" a host church needs most, and instead learn to ask how they can come alongside the host church in their ongoing efforts. Working side by side to address a local community's needs—buoying up weary local leaders and adding manpower to their ministries and initiatives—will almost always be the way to create sustainable solutions.

A more subtle form of the inequality between sending and host churches often shows up in the scheduling of STMs. Most of these trips get

3. Greer and Smith, *Created to Flourish*, 20.

scheduled according to the travelers's needs, not the host church's needs; the majority of trips understandably occur during the United States summer season, when students are out of schools and parents can take vacation. But this arrangement too often places a burden on the host church, which ends up making a lot of sacrifices to accommodate incoming teams. As the host team, we have to put aside other major church or community endeavors to concentrate on the mission teams and their activities, which are often not actually aligned with our church interests or goals. Having a run of teams visiting at the same time, or week after week all through the United States summer season, causes extensive disruptions to our local church ministry and to local community members's livelihoods.

One further caution might be offered on this topic; in our experience, some sending churches use short-term trips as a way to develop their young people and encourage their interests. Missions can be a wonderful and healthy opportunity for discipleship of this kind, but it's truly healthy only if done within the context of attention to the real needs of the host church, sensitivity to the local culture, and an authentic desire for equality. As hosts, we want to see short-termers come into our context with questions and a desire to listen, not just with their own interests and team-building needs in mind.

Focusing on the Good

An Asset-based Approach to Short-term Missions

STEVE CORBETT AND MEGAN PRATT

IT'S IMPORTANT TO RECOGNIZE that STMs are a relatively recent product of the last thirty years. Historically, becoming a "missionary" meant committing to a vocation of living and serving abroad. A "short-term" approach to missions then, was previously defined by a commitment of several years. However, western evangelical churches began to redefine "short-term mission trips" as one to two weeks, largely focused on "doing good" and "seeing change happen in the participants." In this new model, poverty alleviation work eventually has become a primary motive, and that is certainly true of STMs today.

The problem is that, when poverty alleviation becomes the primary goal, it becomes easy to make unthinking assumptions that people experiencing poverty essentially need things *brought to* or *done for* them. STMs then often include projects; for the poor we paint churches, build cinderblock houses, and dig wells. To those we deem needy, we pass out toothbrushes, backpacks, and shoes. What is problematic about these kinds of responses is that they are largely rooted in a western, *material* definition of poverty. When we categorize people by the things they lack, we end up doing more harm than good. As relatively wealthy outsiders serve and give, they reify a *provider/receiver* relationship that sends the (usually unintended) message to those on the receiving end that they are essentially deficient, and "less than."

Rethinking the Definition of Poverty

If we seek to reform STM practices, one change that must happen is a fundamental reorientation of the way that sending organizations think about poverty. The way we define poverty shapes the ways we address needs, and a material definition can often do more harm than good. Though material poverty is certainly a very real challenge, those experiencing poverty often define themselves in more psychological and social terms, far more than westerners typically recognize. Rather than focus on the lack of material things only, many among the poor will express feeling shame, inferiority, powerlessness, humiliation, fear, hopelessness, depressions, social isolation and voicelessness. Material responses to poverty on the part of STM teams can end up affirming the guilt and shame those experiencing poverty may feel, robbing them from the divine truth that they are made in the image of a loving God.

Rather than focus on the "deficiencies" of the poor, a better approach would be to look for the strengths and resources already present in a community. Rather than doing things *to* and *for* the poor, this asset-based approach seeks to support appropriate conditions that allow the poor to recognize the inherent strengths in their context, and to become the agents of change needed in their own communities. An asset-based orientation to STM service "is intended to affirm, and to build upon the remarkable work already going on in neighborhoods across the country."[4] The resources that foreigners bring might still be necessary and useful, but *only as they build upon local assets.*

An asset-based orientation however should benefit not just the poor, but also the STM team members who seek to serve. When participants in short-term missions understand the poor more holistically—in terms of needs *and* strengths—it also allows them to *see their own work—and themselves*—in a more honest light. That is because a focus on the deficits of others allows STM visitors to ignore their own brokenness and spiritual poverty. The internal, often unnoticed assumption of inherent superiority that comes from an external focus on the deficiencies of others ultimately creates social walls and erodes the possibility for authentic relationships. In contrast, a strengths-orientation "can help overcome the god-complexes of the outsiders and the feelings of inferiority on the part of the many poor people."[5] In the end, short-term mission practices can be significantly redeemed when both visitor and host understand not just the strengths that each brings to an STM encounter, but also the brokenness they share in common.

Steve Corbett

Steve Corbett is the Community Development Specialist for the Chalmers Center for Economic Development and an Assistant Professor in the Department of Economics and Community Development at Covenant College. Previously, Steve worked for Food for the Hungry International as the Regional Director for Central and South America and as Director of Staff Training. Steve has a

---

4. Kretzmann and McKnight, "Building Communities," 7.
5. Corbett and Fikkert, *When Helping Hurts,* 38.

B.A. from Covenant College and a M.Ed. in Adult Education from the University of Georgia.

Megan Pratt

Serving as Manager of Grassroots Organizing at World Vision, Megan has a passion for mobilizing the church around best practices in global development and advocating for vulnerable children. With a master's degree in International Development, one of her favorite topics of conversation is "helping without hurting" principles and best practices in child protection. She was able to live that out for eleven years at World Vision, leading their Child Ambassador Team, training and resourcing donors as brand ambassadors who advocate and fundraise for vulnerable children. Megan is married to Chris Pratt, and though she's proud of her Alaskan roots, she currently lives in and loves Tacoma, Washington.

Bibliography

Corbett, Steve and Brian Fikkert. *When Helping Hurts: How to Alleviate Poverty without Hurting the Poor . . . and Yourself.* Chicago: Moody, 2014.
Kretzmann, John and John McKnight. "Building Communities from the Inside Out: A Path Toward Finding and Mobilizing a Community's Assets." *The Asset-Based Community Development Institute,* (1993). https://resources.depaul.edu/abcd-institute/publications/Documents/GreenBookIntro%20 2018.pdf.

A Commitment to Candor

The kind of humility and willingness to listen we've described above, however, demands reciprocal commitment from the host church in the form of candor. Candor comes easily for our western brothers and sisters; from our experience with western mission's teams, colleagues, and friends, it seems that even uncomfortable territory is visited in conversation, uncomfortable questions are asked when they need to be, and relationships can progress without any hidden agendas. Within many African cultures, however, there is an inherent fear of hurting others's feelings. This is a particularly great fear when welcoming guests, including visiting mission teams! Our culture trains us to avoid confrontation, so we might deal with difficult or disappointing situations in ways that do not honestly address the root issues or even acknowledge that they exist.

Too often, then, in the context of STMs, an African host church's leaders will suppress their opinions and feelings regarding their expectations of, or experiences with, a mission trip or project for the sake of pleasing their visitors. We may fear losing the partnership or resources if we tell the truth, and thus frame our questions and comments cautiously and never achieve clear, shared expectations. A lot of money and time is misspent simply because the host is not candid and bold enough to give feedback about what may not be working within the short-term teams and their interventions.

A useful example comes from the situation with the water filters we described above. The local community needed a fresh borehole well, but instead they received expensive water filters from a visiting United States missions team. Community members were appreciative of what they were given, but their real need remained unmet because they still did not have a reliable, sustainable source of clean water. The filters were only going to last twelve months and there was no money within the community to replace them! The well-meant visiting team presumably thought, "There is water there, it just needs to be filtered," and because there wasn't honest communication in both directions, they didn't know that what was needed was actually just a cleaner water source. The host community leaders spoke very gratefully while the visitors were there, but as soon as the team left they began to talk amongst themselves about how much better a borehole would have been. Sadly, that feedback was never given to the sending church, and both churches lost out on the chance to build a more authentic, more productive relationship.

Without candor on the part of the host church, even the most careful listening on the part of the sending church will not be effective; any attempts to strengthen a community together in mutually uplifting, long-term ways risk being defeated from the beginning. African ministry leaders (and those from other cultures that traditionally avoid candor) *must* confront this cultural trait in themselves and commit to a culture of candor in the context of short-term missions. A sending church will never know about problems or even toxicity within their plans and activities unless it is communicated honestly and directly. The sending church can help open communication lines by specifically requesting honest feedback and being sensitive to the possibility of cultural differences that might make their hosts feel unable to be candid, but the responsibility is on the host church to choose candor no matter how uncomfortable it may feel.

We and other leaders in our ministries in Rwanda and Zimbabwe are beginning to learn and choose a culture of candor, and to our surprise, we find that sending churches are responding with gratitude! As both host and sending churches approach each other in a posture of equality, honesty, and partnership, they create space for mutual, long-lasting encouragement, and growth. Our prayer is that church leaders in Africa and elsewhere who host STMs will learn to speak the truth in love.

Relational Consistency

The postures of equality, listening, and candor described above can best exist within genuine and committed relationships between sending and host churches. However, such relationships are difficult to build when most short-term travelers will never return twice to the same community. The lack of consistency between teams and sending churches does not allow room for cultural understanding, meaningful relationships, and clear expectations to grow. What does often grow is frustration. In an inconsistent partnership, the host church will likely engage in certain activities only when teams are on the ground. When the team leaves, those activities in the host community also stop, and until and unless there's a next trip, no follow-up communication may take place from either party. This can be frustrating to many on both sides who are passionate about serious ministry and want to see long-term results of their efforts. A healthy alternative is for a sending church and host church to commit to partnering together long-term, so that trust, shared expectations, project plans and reporting, and cultural understanding can be developed over time.

Within such a long-term relationship, practical steps can be taken to avoid some of the traditional pitfalls of STMs described above. For example, after dealing with the disruptions from badly scheduled mission trips too many times, we saw the need to address expectations and logistics with both the sending church and our host churches well in advance of team travel. We began holding a series of meetings with sending pastors, team members, and host church pastors long before each team arrived on the ground. We have also learned to take advantage of post-trip evaluations and the opportunity they offer to highlight concerns and offer candid feedback after travelers return home. Thanks to early preparation and after-the-fact conversations, we have begun to see real change in the way our visiting short-term teams plan. There is an increase in listening and inquiry, and a growing spirit of collaboration. Today, our visiting teams and our local ministry teams are truly allied on behalf of a shared purpose—a purpose we share as coequal members of one global church.

Needs assessments conducted by host churches independently—or in collaboration and cooperation with sending churches—offer another practical way to create shared understanding. These assessments bring clarity to the needs and expectations of the local community and can help partners to formulate sustainable, homegrown solutions together. Such an approach allows the short-term team and the sending church to feel that they're involved in work that matters, while ensuring that the *actual* needs of the local community are met and not overridden. It also helps to ensure that whatever activities occur during a short-term trip are not unnecessarily disruptive to community members's work and lives, and are not simply designed to fill a team's time. All of this can be accomplished when a commitment to candor is partnered with relational consistency.

The Way Forward for Mutual Transformation

What we've sought to show in this chapter is the potential for community development, mutual encouragement, and global church transformation that exists within a reimagined form of STM. It all begins with asking how churches can serve and encourage each other as partners in Christ's global work, rather than focusing on who has resources and who lacks them. Next, it involves sending churches and short-term teams choosing to *come alongside* their host churches, not intervening or fixing them. This posture alone will help set the stage for healthier, more honest partnerships. Host churches, meanwhile, must be aware of their own needs, propose solutions within their context, and maintain open communication and candor about potential missions activities or initiatives. As sending and hosting churches form longer-term partnerships, they will together create the safety of authentic relationship needed to learn together, grow together spiritually, and build strong long-term strategies and solutions together to address community needs.

The challenges within STM are real, but they can be overcome through mindset shifts and cultural adjustments on both sides. Changing long-embedded cultural attitudes is not easy, but we believe that churches can turn to Scripture and the Holy Spirit for help in shaping and transforming their own behaviors and attitudes as they learn to serve each other with grace and respect. And as individual and partnering churches are transformed, transformation may well take place within the STM institution as a whole. Short-term trips designed within authentic partnerships, constructed on a foundation of equality, and implemented through loving and open communication can play a life-giving role in the sending church and the host church. Such missions position both to be catalysts of holistic, sustainable transformation in their communities and in the global church, and they bring glory to the God who created and loves every tribe, nation, and people equally.

Emmanuel Karegyesa

Emmanuel Karegyesa is a Pastor with the Anglican Church of Rwanda in Kigali Diocese and a community development practitioner with HOPE International in the East and Central Africa Region.

Tom Rakabopa

Tom Rakabopa serves on the Missions Committee of Central Baptist Church—Harare, Zimbabwe, and is the Training and Spiritual Integration Coordinator for HOPE Zimbabwe Trust.

Emily Carminati

Emily is a communications expert, community development practitioner, and writer working in an international ministry setting. She finds many ways to combine her passions for cross-cultural learning, telling stories in ways that honor, and building copowering partnerships that lead to transformation.

Bibliography

Greer, Peter and Phil Smith, *Created to Flourish: How Employment-based Solutions Help Eradicate Poverty,* HOPE International, 2016.

3

The Mutuality Motivation

Jay Matenga

To reimagine what short-term missions could become, we would do well to consider the mutual benefits that emerge when people from different cultural backgrounds interact. Chief among them is the intercultural transformation that comes as a result of participating in relationships of difference. Intercultural transformation is a type of personal development within the context of cross-cultural relationships that can expand our understanding of the world and lead to a deep sense of fulfillment from the connectivity we experience. What happens because of the relational interplay in cross-cultural encounters is a kind of blending, a hybridization of the personalities involved, where the hosts and their environments start to shape the visitors, and the visitors and their ideas begin to re-form the indigenous hosts. It is reciprocated influence: copowerment that changes everyone and, over time, forms a mutuality of belonging.

Why do people visit foreign lands? The answers are many and complex, but there are a fairly narrow set of motivators that encourage Christians from what I call "industrial" contexts (individualist, western, Global North or First World) to visit "indigenous" ones (collectivist, Global South,

Majority World, Developing or Second and Third Worlds).[1] We have seen short-term trips multiply since the mid-nineties, accelerated by cheap and easily arranged international travel. But travel is an enabler, not necessarily a motivator. Peer pressure can be a motivator, but not a healthy one. A desire to help other people can be good and fruitful too when done well, but tends to be a superficial motivator. When we pull back the spiritual veneer of short-term trip engagement, I believe the prime underlying motivator, particularly for younger people since the turn of the century, is a desire for self-development and fulfillment.

Becoming Better People

The pursuit of self-development and fulfillment is not necessarily wrong. It can be a worthy motivator if it is not an end in itself. The purpose of our personal development should be to increase our capacity to contribute positively to the world—to be a blessing to others. Furthermore, as followers of Jesus, we must never forget that we cannot achieve lasting fulfillment apart from him and his purposes. The broader desire to develop ourselves and establish our identity is now an integrated part of the fabric of our reality, especially for those privileged to live in contexts that enjoy more freedom of choice. The philosopher Charles Taylor has labelled our current era as the age of authenticity, and the search for the "authentic self" could be seen as the undercurrent driving cultural change that has been happening all over the world in the latter half of the twentieth and early twenty-first centuries.[2]

This self-development or fulfillment dynamic not only applies to individualistic industrials. People with indigenous backgrounds gain in this environment too. Along with others, group-oriented people are enjoying new freedoms to assert themselves. Indigenous values and customs

---

1. I use the term "indigenous" to refer to people groups who see themselves as connected to others by default, as an integrated part of the physical and spiritual world around them. They tend to relate to the world in terms of intimately interconnected relationships, and terms such as family, covenants, guardianship, hospitality, honor, generosity, harmony, etc. In contrast, people in "individualist" contexts assume they exist separate from most others and their environments, and are autonomous. They tend to relate to the world as a system of connections between independent bodies. They use terms such as teams, partners, contracts, ownership, transactions, law, profit, productivity, *et cetera*.

2. Taylor, *Secular Age*.

are increasingly being seen, heard, validated, and protected in industrial societies around the world (but not without resistance). This has encouraged indigenous people elsewhere to guard their cultural perspectives with more confidence. There is a growing expectation of self-determination, and increased resistance to cultural imposition from outsiders on the one hand, and extraction and appropriation by outsiders on the other. Distaste of outsiders imposing their view upon a group has developed to the point of being considered highly immoral over the past few decades. This is proving a challenge to traditional concepts of world evangelization. Resistance against uninvited influence may be on the increase but it need not be a bad thing. Resistance creates tension and it is in the contexts of tension that mutual transformation can happen. Evangelists and missionaries need to innovate new ways of witnessing to the gospel that are co-operative rather than impositional—ways that are co-created in the midst of the tensions.

Intercultural Transformation

In my Māori cultural environment, visitors are typically embraced and highly regarded as a source of new knowledge. The initial interaction between visitors (*manuhiri*) and hosts (*tangatawhenua*) is considered a sacred occasion, and there are well-defined protocols that guide the meeting of the two peoples. The customary introduction process is called a **pōwhiri**, which conveys the idea of weaving (*whiriwhiri*) two realities together out of ignorance (*pō, darkness*) toward enlightenment or mutual understanding. The bringing together of the two peoples in an interactive context of co-creating understanding of one another benefits both the visitors and the hosts. The process varies in the amount of time involved, but when there is a mutual sense of common understanding, the formalities are concluded with the pressing of noses (a mingling of breath/life force, bringing peace) and a communal meal. From that point forward, the visitors are considered family and they are afforded all the privileges of the tribe . . . and held accountable as members also—sometimes a challenging responsibility, but you certainly learn quickly!

Mutual, intercultural transformation is most powerfully experienced at points of tension in relationships. Often, we imagine that relational harmony is the absence of disagreement, but that is an illusion. Just as you cannot produce a harmonic on an instrument string without tuned tension, so it is with creating harmony in groups. Harmony is not possible without holding the tension. It is within the tensions of difference that creativity emerges. The more diverse the participants, the more severe the tensions of difference, and the greater the benefit for all if the tensions are tuned well. The benefits can be many, but the personal development potential within the creative interaction should be highly valued. We are literally "transformed by the renewing of our minds" through this process of mutual interaction.[3] So, personal or self-development happens in the context of interpersonal tensions, not in the absence of them.

Although the phrase quoted above is lifted from Romans 12:2, being transformed is not specifically Christian. It is common to all human experience. It is what shapes our identities and forms our unique personhood. The scientific discipline of interpersonal neurobiology confirms this dynamic. Christian psychologist, Dr. Curt Thompson notes that, "The interactions within interpersonal relationships deeply shape and influence the development of the brain; likewise, the brain and its development shape and influence those very same relationships."[4] In short, our neural pathways are constantly formed through our interactions with others. We are shaped daily as people by who and what we expose ourselves to. Even more so if those interactions are with people of a different background from us, like those you meet on a short-term trip. The fact that our relationships create us as people is part of what it means to grow as vulnerable humans. When Christians interact together the added factor of being in Christ and empowered by the Holy Spirit, adds a spiritual development dimension to the process. It is all part of our journey of development as disciples of Christ in our communities of faith.

The Challenge of the New

When we are confronted with something new, we are deeply challenged and are driven to reconcile the new information with our current way of understanding the world—to seek resolution. That can come in the form of arrogant resistance or dismissive ignorance because we cannot find a point of commonality, so the new information is perceived as either irrelevant or, at worst, a threat. Alternatively, it can be met with humility and curious openness, seeing the encounter as having potential to enlarge our view and understanding of the world. This has particular relevance to long

3. Rom 12:2 (NIV)
4. Thompson, *Anatomy of the Soul*, 6.

and short-term cross-cultural encounters alike. As intercultural specialist
Joseph Shaules notes,

> *Foreign experiences make possible a process of deep cultural learn-*
> *ing,* one that can make us aware of the cultural configuration of
> our unconscious mind, and make us more effective interculturally.
> This learning process can be experienced in negative ways—such
> as culture shock or cross-cultural misunderstanding—but it also
> can stimulate personal growth and provoke deep-seated changes
> in our perception, worldview, and identity.[5]

Positive transformation and growth happen when we allow ourselves to
be affected. In many ways our mind (the core of our being, which includes
but extends beyond our thought processes) grows like a muscle with the
breaking down and the rebuilding of relevance. Note Shaules's reference to
identity; intercultural experiences help our authentic self to grow.

Princeton educationalist James Loder recognized that we learn, grow,
and are enlarged as people by experiences that challenge our prior understanding of the world around us. He viewed learning and self-development
as a kind of trauma or resolution process.[6] As with any traumatic experience
we do not leave the encounter unchanged and, if it is processed well, we are
often better off. Richard Tedeschi, a leading researcher into post-traumatic
growth, claims, "As many as ninety percent of survivors experience at least
one form of posttraumatic growth, such as a renewed appreciation for life or
a deeper connection to their heart's purpose"[7]. Dwelling with people from
different backgrounds from ourselves, even for a short amount of time, may
seem minor compared to a major life crisis, but it is a traumatic experience,
nonetheless. When our understanding of the world is challenged, we need
to process the experience through to resolution. Assuming the resolution
we arrive at is one of embrace and not exclusion, we become a little more
interculturally adapted as a person than we were before the encounter—our
authentic self develops in unique ways. Once this happens and becomes a
means for blessing those around us, it is wonderfully fulfilling and, therefore,
a beneficial outcome from cross-cultural encounters—for visitors and hosts.

5. Shaules, *Intercultural Mind,* 17.

6. Loder, *Transforming Moment.*

7. Haas, *Bouncing Forward,* 3.

Reciprocated Relationship

The apostle James testified, "Consider it pure joy, my brothers and sisters, whenever you face trials of many kinds, because you know that the testing of your faith produces perseverance. Let perseverance finish its work so that you may be mature and complete, not lacking anything."[8] The testing James referred to was not external, such as persecution. Rather, in the context of the letter, James was referring to the tensions (testing, trial, temptations) between the rich and the poor, the privileged and the marginalized, *within* the fellowship.

In any given interpersonal Christian interaction, the principle from James applies: persevere in the difficulties, hold onto the fact that we are of one faith, and you will grow in maturity as a disciple of Christ . . . needing nothing. That ought to evoke joy! It is a promise of fulfillment that comes from dwelling together in reciprocated relationship—a mutuality of belonging. It is not an easy process of development, and it is further amplified when the interpersonal relationships are intercultural, across boundaries of difference. Yet the benefits of growth for all are well worth the investment in the change process.

In view of the many humanitarian and environmental challenges the world faces today, the global church has a great opportunity to collaborate and co-create solutions—as an organic whole, interconnected in Christ (as in 1 Cor 12:12–26). Solutions can flow both ways, from the industrial to the indigenous and indigenous to the industrial, as we each acknowledge our limitations and welcome the strengths in each others's perspectives, allowing the mutual learning experience to develop us as people and disciples. Fulfillment comes from allowing the love of Christ to compel us to contribute to the wellbeing of those with whom we have a relationship, and to be open to where the Spirit wants us to collaborate beyond existing relationships—especially to the family of faith, but not exclusively.[9] Whether short-term or long-term, as we join together across boundaries in transformative relationships and work together for the betterment of the world around us, everyone should be changed and blessed in the copowerment process. This is the principle of mutuality. This is God's love in action, and it glorifies God. Rather than fulfilment for our own self's sake, expressing our integrated loving unity toward mutual fulfilment must become the prime

8. James 1:3–4 (NIV).

9. Galatians 6:10 (ESV).

motivator for reaching across boundaries and borders. Only then will the world believe and know that the Father lovingly sent the Son.[10]

Jay Matenga

Jay Matenga is a Māori theologian of missions practice who serves as the Director of the World Evangelical Alliance Global Witness Department and Executive Director of its Mission Commission. Jay's M.A. from All Nations Christian College explored mission groups through a post-modern lens and his doctorate from Fuller School of Mission and Theology developed this theme in post-coloniality. Drawing on his indigenous background, Jay believes that mutuality is the way forward for missions in diversity.

Bibliography

Haas, Michaela. *Bouncing Forward: The Art and Science of Cultivating Resilience.* New York: Simon and Schuster, 2016.
Loder, James E. *The Transforming Moment.* 2nd ed. Colorado Springs: Helmers and Howard, 1989.
Shaules, Joseph. *The Intercultural Mind: Connecting Culture, Cognition, and Global Living.* Boston: Intercultural, 2015.
Taylor, Charles. *A Secular Age.* Cambridge, MA: Harvard University Press, 2007.
Thompson, Curt. *Anatomy of the Soul: Surprising Connections between Neuroscience and Spiritual Practices That Can Transform Your Life and Relationships.* Carol Stream, IL: Tyndale House, 2010.

10. John 17:18–26 (NIV).

4

Restorying Short-Term Trips
From McMission to Mutuality

RYAN KUJA

CARL JUNG, THE ICONIC father of analytic psychology, is credited with saying, "Until you make the unconscious conscious, it will direct your life and
you will call it fate." Jung, with his keen acumen for reaching into and un-
earthing the depths of the human psyche and soul—that of his patients as
well as his own—recognized that operative within each person are forces,
undetected and unnoticed, which exert influence on our choices and guide
our lives. Jesus recognized something similar. Though he used language
appropriate to the Hebrew worldview of the Ancient Near East as opposed
to Jung's mid-twentieth century European psychodynamic lingo, Jesus was
a master of pointing out the subtleties, the obscure, the hidden, the things
that are difficult to discern. He named the factors that kept people bound
to painful states of being, to falsity, to ego, to violence and everything that
robs life, everything that thwarts the in-breaking of the kingdom of God.

In the Gospel of Luke, Jesus says, "For there is nothing hidden that
will not be disclosed, and nothing concealed that will not be known or
brought out into the open."[1] Bringing what is recessed and covered up into

---

1. Luke 8:17 (NIV).

the light is a fundamental task Jesus followers are called to. If we are to move away from expressions of mission that create unintentional harm—and simultaneously reimagine STMs in ways that allow us to embody the gospel across cultures in more beautiful ways—this is a process that the gospel is inviting us into.

The Stories that Shape Us

Human beings are creatures of story. We make sense of the world and our experiences through narrative. Stories are powerful shapers of how we see God, others, and ourselves. Each of us have narratives within us—often unconscious, concealed, and undisclosed—that impact the particular ways we engage in STM trips. In fact, some of the narratives alive within us—individually as missionaries and collectively as churches, sending agencies, and the broader evangelical culture in North America—are contrary to the *missio Dei*, God's mission.

Any service trips that we participate in should, if they are to be worthy of the name "mission" or "Christian," be in alignment with God's mission of restoration, flourishing for all of the created order, and *shalom*—everything in right relationship with everything else, which is what the kingdom of God expresses. A central part of the work of reimagining STM is becoming aware of the deeper narrative realm that manifests itself in the particular ways we engage in economically marginalized communities in the Majority World that are in dissonance with God's mission—methods and practices that create dependency, reinforce self-blame on the economically poor, and perpetuate neocolonialism.

For the purposes of this chapter, I'd adapt Jung's words above: until we have awareness of the stories hidden within us, they will direct how we do mission and we will call them God. This work of awareness is a process that begins from the inside out. Developing fluency in "reading" the narratives that guide us is vital—lest we fall into the trap of accidentally calling them God. The North American church is in desperate need of a better story about what short-term mission is and what it has the potential to be. Critical reflection on these guiding narratives is a difficult but necessary aspect of re-storying STM. Addressing methods alone—while largely neglecting the deeper narrative realm—has yielded thin modifications rather than deep, innovative change in terms of how we think about and engage in short-term trips. The church is in need not only of a corrective for the subtle disempowering narratives that guide us, but also of an invitation to unleash a new missional imagination that will lead to robust innovation in how we engage cross-culturally.

The SAD State of McMission

In general, STM trips tend to reflect western culture more than the gospel message, with a focus on completing tasks and accomplishing goals—often goals the team has set without truly listening to the ones they ostensibly seek to serve. There is a prioritization of *product* over *process*. In terms of human connection, such trips yield a veneer of chumminess over a commitment to authentic, long-term relationships. Approaches that truly empower the real experts on issues of poverty and injustice—the local leaders—are often eschewed in favor of heeding our own agendas and meeting our own aims.

You may have heard the term Standard American Diet (SAD), a modern, western way of eating that includes a glut of nutritionless, highly processed food (or more accurately, food-like substances) such as candy, refined grains, and trans fats.[2] They taste good and are quite convenient, involving little time or effort in terms of preparation. And who doesn't love some fries from the drive-thru window? Correspondingly, North Americans taking part in short-term trips tend to peddle a sort of STM version of the SAD—one characterized by a fast-food approach, and motivated by habits of speed and hustle. At first glance these methods appear to be wholesome, nourishing for us and those we are serving; they taste great and offer immediate satisfaction and gratification. But over the long term, the SAD version of STM practice inevitably leads to dis-ease.

In keeping with the food metaphor, this SAD diet of STM is a characteristic of what I call "McMission." It involves the culturally-construed beliefs, perceptions, and norms adopted by western Christians which unintentionally perpetuate systems of injustice in the Majority World. Since beliefs, perceptions, and norms are all rooted in deeper narratives—and since narratives largely operate below the level of our conscious awareness—the foundations of McMission operate at a deep, subterranean level. As Jung said, we must make the unconscious conscious. Doing that work means first becoming aware of it; only then can we begin to examine it closely and with care . . . not with contempt but with curiosity. The purpose of deconstructing McMission isn't a resignation to cynicism or blame; nor

2. For more on SAD and McMission, see Kuja, *Inside Out*, 45–61.

is deconstruction an excuse to do nothing at all. Rather, critique arises from love; we do the work of deconstructing in order to "do good better." We do this work because we realize it isn't optional if we are to participate in STM in ways that truly honor the dignity of the ones we seek to serve in our short-term endeavors; we do this work in order to align our service with God's mission. As we interrogate the narratives that sustain injustice, a space is created in which something new can be constructed. This space is pregnant with the possibility of re-storying—that is, creating new narratives that can guide us into innovative STM approaches rooted in the gospel rather than McMission.

Culture and Context

A number of years ago while serving as a missionary in South Africa, I was sitting around a campfire talking with some new friends. One of the guys was animatedly telling the story of a break-in at his house:

> The family was so clever. The adults sent the babies through the window of my house! he exclaimed excitedly. Then the little ones opened the doors and the whole crew got in. They raided the cabinets, threw flour all over the place, ate everything in sight, and defecated on the couches. It was an awful mess!

I could hardly believe what I was hearing. How could parents do something like that? Use their children to break into a house and wreak such havoc? What I eventually realized is that I had missed a very key detail in the story: the characters of the story weren't people. They were baboons! I was lacking the vital information of the story: the context.

You probably hear the word "context" on a regular basis. But what does it really mean? Essentially, context has to do with background, setting, and circumstances. I like to think of it as the thing beneath the thing. Religion. Values. Worldview. Relationships. Context is everything. The biblical text emphasizes the importance of context, nowhere more so than with the apostle Paul. When he traveled to Athens to share the gospel with the Greeks, Paul didn't just show up and announce a message divorced from their cultural context. Instead, he framed his message using Greek philosophy and ideas so that people could better understand and resonate with his message.[3]

---

3. Kuja, *Inside Out*, 104–8.

As polytheists, the pagan Greeks worshipped a number of different gods including Zeus and Poseidon. In Acts 17:28, Paul draws on their religious texts to explain that God was the ground of all being and the source of existence itself: "For in him we live and move and have our being. As some of your own poets have said, 'We are his offspring.'"[4] The Athenians could understand that type of religious paradigm. It made sense to them and meshed with their cosmology and worldview. Paul was able to powerfully relay the gospel message to the Greeks because he honored the importance of context.

So why wasn't Paul captive to the very human habit of engaging those from different cultures through the narrow lens of his own? Simply put, Paul had cultural intelligence. He understood his own cultural locatedness, and the locatedness of those he was ministering to, and took both into account. Without cultural intelligence, Paul's message would have been parochial and impotent, devoid of contextual relevance. His preaching could even have even resulted in the perpetuation of cultural imperialism—one of the things Jesus taught his disciples to abstain from.[5]

Learning Ourselves

One of the main drivers of the McMission approach—that often hidden element of contemporary STM practice that has to be "brought out into the open"—is our failure to understand the cultural contexts of the communities we visit. Generally speaking, a robust process of studying the intricate nuances of cultural context is rarely part of the STM preparation and formation process. Yet even if it were, engaging in the work of developing cultural intelligence is more complex than committing to a dynamic and comprehensive study *only of the cultures we visit.* Just as important (and just as neglected) is the need to study the culture of *ourselves.*

Culture doesn't simply exist "out there" in the world. It is also "in here"—the stories culture tells us that create the narrative framework through which we see ourselves and make sense of the world. Sadly, though, people from dominant cultures tend to have a difficult time understanding their own cultural particularities and locatedness because they tend to see themselves as culturally neutral; and that insidious mindset prevents them

---

4. Acts 17:28 (NIV).

5. Kuja, *Inside Out*, 81–85.

from seeing that in fact all people enact the values and behaviors of their own culture contexts.[6]

The deep culture stories on which most white American evangelicals were raised place tremendous value on performance, achievement, and "doing God's work." Correspondingly, the American cultural narrative de-emphasizes relationship and "being"—as opposed to rescuing others and "doing." An important part of the narrative that informs short-term mission trips is all about the nobility of helping people in need (usually brown and black people who live in different countries). This message, however covert or overt, tells us that dark-skinned, economically poor people are more or less passively waiting for white-skinned, relatively wealthy people to arrive and help or save them. This is a core feature of McMission that must be brought into the light, for as long as it remains in the dark it will continue to promote the paternalism and a white savior mentality that make current STM practices fundamentally unjust.

If there is any hope for a reimagined alternative to the current STM status quo, we must become aware of our own cultural narratives, and to acknowledge the ways in which they shape our engagement in short-term missions. Only then do we stand a chance at creating fundamentally different approaches that resist the destructive assumptions of McMission. And this we must do, for the sake of the gospel, and for the sake of the dignity of those we serve.

A Conversion to Exquisite Mutuality

For those who seek the reform of short-term missions practices, there is another aspect of self-understanding by which we might resist McMission: a commitment to knowing and embracing our own brokenness that we share in common with all people. Such a commitment means interrogating those elements of our cultural story that lets us believe that—because we are wealthy, or white, or "developed"—or even "saved," that we somehow, inherently stand above those who are the objects of our missional efforts. Yet the human condition—regardless of where we are culturally located in the world—is one of suffering. No one escapes pain in this life, and no one is completely whole. Becoming cognizant that our shared humanity is to be found in brokenness means that, rather than hiding our wounds, we can lead with our wounds as Jesus did. The process of recognizing our own

6. Kuja, *Inside Out*, 98.

brokenness allows us to engage with others from a stance of humility and coequality. The goal of STM shifts from an objectifying zeal to serve or save, into a commitment to accompany others as wounded healers.

By re-storying ourselves in this way, we are freed to offer our wounded selves to those who are also wounded. Author and priest Fr. Gregory Boyle writes, "We are not invited to rescue, fix or save people. The heart of ministry is to receive people and then enter into the exquisite mutuality God intends for us all."[7] Exquisite mutuality represents the communion, kinship, and solidarity that is a possibility when the hierarchy between the so called "whole" and the so called "broken" disintegrates. Boyle goes on to write, "We cannot turn the light switch on for anyone. But we all own flashlights. With any luck, on any given day, we know where to aim them for each other. We do not rescue anyone at the margins. But go figure, if we stand at the margins, we are all rescued. No mistake about it."[8] Adopting Boyle's idea of exquisite mutuality as a more authentically biblical narrative foundation for STM means that missional service also becomes an opportunity for short-term team members to be converted—to see themselves afresh, to learn to see the "other" with new eyes, and even to see the gospel anew as it is expressed in new cultural contexts.

The echo of Jesus's insight in his words in Luke's Gospel and the reverberations of Jung's counsel lead us to insights that go beyond the psychological realm and into the heart of the gospel itself, the good news that is ever inviting us to unmask, unveil, and reimagine for the sake of the Kingdom of God. By making the unconscious conscious, and by bringing to light that which has been concealed, we can begin to re-story mission from the inside out, releasing collective re-imagination and generating innovative praxis centered on mutual transformation of the "server" and the "served" alike.

Ryan Kuja

Ryan Kuja is a trauma-informed therapist and spiritual director. With a background in international mission, relief, and development, he is a global

7. Salai, "Saving Gang Members from the Street," https://www.americamagazine.org/faith/2014/08/20/saving-gang-members-street-qa-father-greg-boyle-sj.

8. Boyle, "Thought I Could Save Gang Members," https://www.americamagazine.org/faith/2017/03/28/father-greg-boyle-i-thought-i-could-save-gang-members-i-was-wrong.

citizen who has lived in fifteen cities on five continents. Ryan holds two master's degrees from The Seattle School of Theology and Psychology (MA Theology and Culture) and Grand Rapids Theological Seminary (MA Clinical Mental Health Counseling). His writing has been published in a variety of peer-reviewed journals as well as at *Sojourners, Red Letter Christians,* and *Missio Alliance.* His book, *From the Inside Out: Reimagining Mission, Recreating the World,* examines global mission through the lens of trauma studies, contextual theology, intercultural competency, and spiritual formation. Ryan lives in Holland, MI, with his wife, Katie, and their toddler triplets.

Bibliography

Boyle, Gregory. "I Thought I Could 'Save' Gang Members. I Was Wrong." *American Magazine* (2017).

Kuja, Ryan. *From the Inside Out: Reimagining Mission, Recreating the World.* Eugene, OR: Cascade, 2018.

Salai, Sean. "Saving Gang Members from the Street? Q & A with Father Greg Boyle, SJ." *The Jesuit Review* (2014).

Discussion Questions

THE FOLLOWING QUESTIONS ARE *meant to create "conversation" between this section's themes and your own perspectives and experiences. They are intended to be useful for both sides of the STM relationship: guests who travel to serve other communities, and the hosts who receive them. While these questions offer thought-provoking prompts for journaling, meditation, and prayer, they also serve as starting places for group discussion with others in your community who care about reimagining STM. We highly recommend both modes of engagement when that is possible.*

1. Describe some examples of power inequality on either side of the STM equation. What is behind these imbalances? How do they constrain collaboration? How do they work against dynamics of coequality? Take a moment to review the definition of *copowerment* in chapter one; then, take some time to imagine alternative, more copowering ways of engaging our sisters and brothers in the global church.

2. While in a perfect world everyone would say what they mean and mean what they say, in reality people often avoid potentially uncomfortable conversations, regardless of how essential they may be. What are potential obstacles to candor between hosts and their STM guests, and what practices might be put into place to facilitate candor? Is this dynamic something that could be discussed with your counterparts in the STM relationship?

3. Whether we send teams or host them, we need to look honestly at our motivations—and that can make us uncomfortable. List the main motives that come to mind when thinking about engaging in short-term missions. Then take some time to think and pray, and later revisit the list to see if there are any less obvious motives that you might not have been aware of before. Are there any particular essays from this section that help you to evaluate and rethink your reasons for supporting STM?

4. Jay Matenga writes that "It is within the tensions of difference that creativity emerges." In your direct experiences, or from stories you have heard about STM, have "differences" been viewed as mostly positive or mostly negative? In STM dynamics, what might cause people to downplay differences? Can you think of situations when the acknowledgement and embrace of differences have (or could have) yielded new perspectives or innovations?

5. Ryan Kuja calls upon us to understand our own cultural stories, specifically so that we can understand and appreciate differences between cultural contexts. What are some defining elements of your own cultural story? Your organization's culture? Your national culture? How might these stories serve as obstacles to authentic mutuality with people of different cultures? How might they be engaged in ways that promote greater understanding for both senders and receivers?

6. One of the points of the essay "Reframing Short-term Missions" is that true relationships require time to grow, develop, and mature. How can we reconcile this need for time with the "short" aspect of short-term missions?

SECTION TWO

Humility and Repentance

ALL CHURCHES ENGAGED IN short-term missions need to face squarely and honestly the past mistakes committed in the name of "mission." Even when there is no direct connection or personal responsibility for historical trans-gressions, Christians can still seek forgiveness and reconciliation on behalf of the church, whether committed in the distant past or in more recent history. There are times when both sending and host cultures are complicit in play-ing out persistent dynamics of colonialism, political disparity, and economic inequality. We must actively and courageously confront, critique, and decon-struct those global-historical forces if we are to find a new way forward.

Therefore, we offer the various essays in this book as, among other things, examples of what the practice of humility looks like when it comes to rethinking short-term missions. The authors in this book model *humility* in that their essential stance toward STM assumes that they *simply know that they don't know all the answers;* they offer new ideas as possibilities rather than definitive conclusions; they acknowledge that, at best, they contribute only part of what will ultimately be a more complex and com-prehensive response to the problems with short-term missions. They have embraced the reality that old ways of doing short-term trips and projects do not work anymore. In fact, many would ask whether past approaches ever really worked well to achieve the church's objectives, and others question the very objectives themselves. And this means that there is a willingness on the part of all stakeholders in the STM industry to admit past failures, to *repent* of mistakes that have caused harm, and to earnestly confess their need for wisdom from many parts of the global church as we try to figure out together where we go from here.

The following chapters highlight this need for repentance and humility in a way that encourages each of us to reexamine our part in STM. For those who would dare to reinvent STM, there are no sacred cows, and no traditions that cannot be questioned. The position of this text assumes that if we are ever to sort out the future of STM praxis, we must begin from this place of letting go of what we think we know. An uncomfortable place, really, of dis-orientation and unknowing—but a necessary one.

5

The Principal of Standing in the Back

Danilo Cyruis, Clelie Cyrius, Stephanie
Robinson, *and* David Sanon, *with* Andrea Sielaff

In the story of missions, who are the central characters? Are the central characters the people local to the mission area or the short-term missionaries? When reading a book or watching a television series, it is usually easy to tell who the central characters are. They are there at the beginning of the narrative, and they are there through the end. Their strengths and challenges are the meat of the plot; their culture creates the tone; their land is usually the setting. Other characters may influence the direction of the story, but they come and go, only present when their personal story arc intersects with those of the central characters and setting.

As the leaders of Konbit Haiti, a faith-based NGO that was co-founded by Americans and Haitians together, we assert that the people local to the mission context should always be the central characters of the story of the mission.[1] For missions to be sustainable and fruitful, the perceived heroes must be the people who are native to the culture and committed for the long-term. Unfortunately, many people who travel to

---

1. *Konbit* is a word drawn from Haitian Creole meaning "working together"

participate in short-term missions are told, both subtly and directly, that they are heroes of the story.

While we would not want to make light of the generosity of short-termers who give time and energy, we do want to call out the false narrative that makes them the central figure in the story of a local mission. Yes, a short-term missionary is likely to have a very dramatic arc as they encounter a broadening perspective of their faith and worldview. But seeing themselves as the center of the story of the mission encourages a narcissism more akin to a reality television show than to God's grand narrative. The deeper harm in putting short-term missionaries front and center of the story is that it displaces and disempowers the true central characters, the locals.

To counter this false narrative, Konbit Haiti has developed the practical value of "standing in the back," which is a physical representation of a metaphorical stance in humility. "Standing in the back" is an approach to short-term missions that can be used in many contexts, though it was born in a specific one. Konbit Water Program Director David Sanon coined this phrase during a staff debrief about a short-term group that was, both literally and metaphorically, taking center stage in Konbit Haiti's open-air community center. Though it is common for visiting groups to take the stage at the community center to perform a skit, this group had also inadvertently revealed their sense of their centrality to the story—and lack of humility—by sitting at the very front even when not on stage. David noted, "They need to learn to stand in the back." We decided as a mission organization to develop multiple ways to help short-term teams learn to stand in the back. We will detail our methods at the conclusion of the chapter, but first we must share more about the context in which the concept arose.

While the phrase "stand in the back" can apply in a metaphorical way, we came to use this phrase specifically because of the physical way that our own outdoor community center is shaped. Teams of all kinds come to help the local, competent staff of Konbit Haiti achieve their goals of clean drinking water, a summer camp for two-hundred kids, Christmas camp, health care education and clinics, pastors' conferences, and business conferences. Local staff, Haitian community members and short-term teams meet together in the community center. At the front is a large stage with a microphone, often required to talk to the large number of people this community center can attract. Each summer, the teams stand up on the stage to share what they have brought to the community. It is understandable that they must stay up there for a time. What we've noticed, though, is the long-term dynamic between Konbit Haiti's year-round Haitian staff and the short-term foreign team. Over the course of time that the foreign team serves, its members drift toward the seats in the front of the community center, closest to the stage. Even when they are not speaking, the short-term missionaries often assume that they ought to remain in charge and in control, the heroes of the story.

For a host mission to ask their short-term guests to stand in the back instead of seating them in the front seems inhospitable—until you consider Jesus's teaching to the guests at the Pharisee's house in Luke 14. Jesus, noticing the presumptuous way that the guests were choosing the most desirable seats, warned them against claiming for themselves the places of honor. Instead, he advises, guests should learn to choose a lower seat and wait to be invited closer to the action by the host. "For all those who exalt themselves will be humbled," Jesus concludes, "and those who humble themselves will be exalted."[2] Our goal in this approach is not to marginalize short-term teams but to help them find the spiritual posture that they need to partner with long-term locals. The principle of standing in the back has the power to move many short-term missions around the world from a paternalistic stance of empowerment to a truly fruitful partnership with local leaders.

The idea of standing in the back is about much more than a physical location. Short-term team members often feel as if they should have more power than national leaders, that their privilege should give them more authority and their expertise should be taken more seriously than that of nationals. In response to this type of assertive power, Haitians end up standing in the back of the room—literally and figuratively. When this happens, our greatest assets in the mission wind up sitting on the bench, reinforcing the long historical narrative of foreign dominance and the powerlessness of the Haitian people to help themselves.

Colonial Contexts

To fully understand the importance of standing in back in the Haitian and other postcolonial contexts, one must consider the history of foreign involvement in that context. For Haiti, that first foreign involvement, what some might even call the first "mission trip" to Haiti, was with the Spanish conquistadors who came with Columbus. Supported by Christianity in their day, these conquerors took advantage of the native people in the land

2. Luke 14:11 (NIV).

and committed mass genocide through violence and the spread of disease. The colonists then introduced slavery to Haiti so they could continue to extract for themselves the natural resources of the island. As the church voiced its support for slavery, European colonial entitlement and brutal dominance became intertwined with Christianity. That twisted relationship is part of the paternalistic dynamic that plays out today in the relationships between Haitian Christians and foreign short-term missionaries.

Despite this history of colonialism, Haiti achieved independence as a nation in 1804. The Haitians developed a rich and vibrant culture and became the wealthiest nation in the Caribbean in the 1950s. However, Haiti's ability to provide for itself was lost when dictators took power and financial disparity rose. With the increase in poverty in Haiti came an influx of well-intentioned missionaries and NGOs. Thousands of aid organizations in Haiti have created what is known as a "Republic of NGOs" that serve as the unofficial government in many parts of the country. Plainly put, organizations do not simply exist in Haiti, they often play God in Haiti.

This "rule by NGO" is not the ideal it might seem to be. In misguided attempts to help the Haitian people, foreigners have disempowered and occasionally abused Haitians. Crippling poverty still overwhelms the systems. One of the systemic reasons that outside aid has not solved the economic problems is that Haitians are not involved in program planning and development at every level. Many organizations hire Haitians, but only in service to foreign goals. Local buy-in and local input are vital to making programs sustainable, long-lasting, and impactful. Despite that fact, local input is rarely requested or heard. The belief that Haitians have less to offer to their own communities than foreign leadership can offer is entrenched; for example, other organizations have expressed shock that Konbit Haiti is able to be so well run and effective with a leadership team that is mostly Haitian.

Stories of Decentering and a Theological Solution

Sometimes this decentering of Haitians from their own story is subtle, and sometimes it is painfully obvious. Several stories from the experiences of Konbit Family Program Director Clelie Cyrius and Konbit Water Program Director David Sanon illustrate both the subtle and more overt ways that visiting, often white, missionaries act as if they are the heroes of the story.

Clelie Cyrius said, "It's difficult to talk about the ways that [short-term] teams impacted me as a child. I know they brought clothing and treats for children like me. However, they also ignored me at the tables we shared. They wouldn't talk to me, they'd just talk about me and my country. They never stopped to ask us what we could use, only doing what they wanted to do."

When David Sanon was a child, his school hosted many foreign visitors who would come through to see how the dollars they'd contributed had been used. Children were taught from the age of seven or eight that everything would stop if a team of *blancs* (a common phrase for people from the United States) came into the room. David described the teachers instructing the children to stand in a line and sing to welcome them. The children would sing (in English, a language not their own): "I am so glad to see you today! Welcome! I am happy to be with you today! Welcome! I am glad to see you today! Welcome! For the glory of God, I wish you welcome!"

Strikingly, David and his classmates did not know the meanings of the words they were singing. Their own understanding was not important relative to the need to please the visitors. "We had to leave our schoolwork and play with them or participate in the programs they had planned for us," David remembered. Oftentimes, they'd give the children candy and take them to the beach.

Visitors had the opportunity to select children to sponsor and send to school, a way to offset the expenses of running a school on an island. This opportunity was not lost on anyone; David's parents would encourage him to play into this game, saying that he needed to "sing really beautifully for the *blancs* so they will pay for your school fees, ok?" He points to the very sure reasoning for this: life in Haiti is difficult. David noted, "When I was a child, I was always happy when the foreigners would come. We could not wait to meet with them."

David now reflects on that experience in a different way. He now sees the warped theology behind the reason for his happiness: "We grew up with the ideology that *blancs* were a blessing. They were necessary for us to be happy; they were the people who brought us peace." He continued, "We knew *blancs* had money, they had cars, and they had a lot of things we did not have." He remembers believing that foreigners *should* hold this heroic role; the belief was reinforced by "all the films we saw about Jesus Christ. He was always white."

There is paternalism in the patronage of the *blancs* that is theologically troubling. Haitians are often treated as objects of aid, rather than persons created in God's image with their own gifts and agency to contribute. This paternalism is not what Haitians ultimately want or need; Haitians want to do for themselves. A local Haitian seen in charge of a successful mission creates hope within the community, addressing the core ideological and psychological foundations of poverty and oppression. Local leadership is better at discerning what the real needs are in the community.

As an organization, Konbit Haiti aims to help Haitian nationals feel that they are created in the likeness of God. Because "God created man in his own image,"[3] they can actively participate in bringing peace and healing to their communities. Tragically, when short-term missionaries put themselves at the center of the story, that theology is warped: the image of God is mediated through the white body to the black body. Short-term missionaries need to transform this warped perspective. They come not to bear the image of God to a lesser people; they come to bear witness to the image of God already at work in local communities.

As an example of what happens when this distorted theology is lived out by short-term missionaries, consider this dehumanizing experience that David Sanon had with a short-term team. David was working on a contract for a local mission, serving as a translator and driver for a short-term team coming to Haiti for a month. A month is plenty of time for short-term and long-term missionaries to develop a relationship of mutual respect. Instead of taking advantage of this opportunity, the short-term team treated David like a servant, with so little consideration of his personhood that it sometimes put him in harm's way.

David recalls waking up before the sun rose in his town of Montrouis, Haiti, and taking the complicated and unreliable public transit system all the way to the short-term compound in the capital each morning. "No one thought about how I would get to the mission site each morning," he noted. "Their only concern was how I could assist them." Each day, he drove the teams to various locations and translated for them. They'd end the day at the compound and eat dinner. Food is a big part of Haitian culture; it is customary that people dine together, sharing in the day and breaking bread with one another. The short-term team did not think to honor this cultural custom; instead, they ate by themselves, only later thinking to give the Haitian staff their leftovers. "They would go upstairs to eat and bring us what they didn't want," he said. He noted that he and the other Haitian staff had to wait for hours to eat. Oftentimes, the expectation that David would stay late resulted in it being too dark for him to safely get a ride home. He ended

3. Genesis 1:27 (ESV).

58

up in the middle of Port-Au-Prince near some of the most dangerous parts of town, calling people to see if he could stay with them overnight.

The lack of thoughtfulness on the part of the short-term team may have seemed benign to them, but it was wounding to the Haitian staff. They were treated as servants instead of expert partners. They were metaphorically and literally standing in the back, relegated to second-class status. The short-term team members put themselves in the center of the story, communicating the more-than and lesser-than belief in their actions. When this short-term team talked about Haiti, their conversations focused on the poverty of the country, the corruption of the government, and the ways they disagreed with what Haitians had done. Though they knew David spoke English, no one considered what their words communicated to him. These kinds of actions are not only bad manners for guests; they are also an offense to the gospel.

David also experienced this short-term team's disrespect and de-centering of Haitians in their treatment of local children. He remembers driving through a particularly difficult part of town when children began running alongside the vehicle. "Children often do this when they see foreigners in a car," David said. "They are just waving and saying hello." However, this team decided it would be prudent to throw treats out of the moving vehicle to the children, throwing the majority of them on the dirt. David noted that this action communicates that "the children are like dogs, not being worthy to be handed something for them to eat." David believes a better way to handle the situation, if the team wanted to share treats, would be to pull over so they could hand the children the treats.

Standing in the Back: Practices for Successful Short-Term Partnerships

Konbit Haiti knows that short-term missions don't have to be this way; they can be mutually beneficial to both host and guest. We know this with certainty because of the positive partnership that led to the co-founding of Konbit Haiti by Americans and Haitians together. This partnership started as a multinational team that traveled around Haiti teaching missionaries about simple ways to impact the water crisis. Eventually, as that consulting work was fully entrusted to local Haitians, the multinational team realized that this model of local leadership could translate into long-term projects and programs.

This model of local leadership taking center stage has resulted in a wave of successful projects. Over two hundred families have been served; water projects and training have helped over thirty thousand people; and communities are coming together to take ownership of their progress.

For short-term teams to have a fruitful impact, they must work with the hosting community from the inception of the project all the way through, being accountable during the mission trips to take a stance of humility. We're sharing here four practices for successful stand-in-the-back projects.

Partnership in Planning

When short-term teams set their program goals and team culture without partnership from nationals, it sets both sides up for disappointment. When short-term teams work for months on a plan without local input, they are often less willing to deviate, adjust, or make accommodations to that plan when they land. Feeling as if they "deserve" to present, teach, and lead from the front, they make local people feel marginalized by the lack of consideration from team members claiming that they are there to help. At Konbit Haiti, we encourage short-term missionaries to partner with our local cultural brokers from the very inception of the trip. This partnership in planning ought to cover both how the team will spend their time and expectations for the team's posture.

In regards to how short-term teams spend their time, local missionaries can clarify the difference between having an actual, lasting impact and "doing" something tangible that gives short-term teams a temporary sense of accomplishment. In our experience, a significant source of complaints from short-term missionaries come from the expectation that their actions should be the center of the story; they want to "do" something meaningful in their time. When teams say that, what they imply is that they want their time to be used in the way they want, no matter if it actually serves the long-term mission or not. With careful partnership in planning, a team's time can be allocated to activities that serve the long-term goals of the mission while also communicating the rationale behind those decisions.

Planning also needs to address expectations for how teams will interact. Without a proper understanding of expectations, teams are often boisterous, demanding, and offensive. Seeing themselves as the center of the story, short-termers have been offended that the Haitian staff members were not more effusive in praising their work. For example, in a post-trip survey, the short-term teams' biggest complaint was that Konbit Haiti's Haitian staff were not as complementing and accommodating to the team as the short-termers thought they should be, with one participant noting that they expected more because they had "made many sacrifices to be [in Haiti]."[4] The Haitian staff were indeed grateful for the teams's time and sacrifice but did not offer the blatant admiration that the team was hoping to receive individually and corporately. Planning with a cultural broker before the trip can change the paternalistic expectation that anyone helped should be overwhelmingly grateful. In this way, teams can set a tone from the beginning that they are serving for the kingdom of God and not for the praise of others.

Using Language to Shape Expectations

At Konbit Haiti, we've revised how we talk about missions to give short-term teams a healthier understanding of partnership. We use the phrase "vision trip" instead of "mission trip." This approach communicates that the heart of the experience is people physically seeing what is already happening at the Konbit Haiti location rather than them attempting to be the facilitator of ministry. The vernacular behind a vision trip has increased the ability of cultural brokers to speak into the lives of people before they come to the island.

We've also switched from using the word "empowerment" to using "copowerment." While empowerment was an important concept that helped people with privilege begin to understand that they could use that power to benefit the greater good, it implies that the flow of power is unidirectional. One person has power, another does not; the haves give power to the have-nots. The reality of the kingdom of God, however, is that everyone has something to contribute. Though a foreigner may have more money or formal education, the local missionaries have relationships and knowledge about what will and will not work in their contexts. There are no have-nots. No one comes to the table empty-handed.

Short-term teams need to come ready to receive the expertise and leadership of locals. To do this, they may need to be introduced to the language of privilege, especially if they have the beneficiaries of white privilege. Because of the colonial history of missions in Haiti and other places, humility has become an essential part of doing life and ministry together; for foreign team members, that attitude of humility often starts

4. Konbit Haiti, post-trip evaluation, 2017.

with acknowledging their own privilege. Though it is helpful to learn more about the ways that this privilege has aided them, it doesn't do anyone any good to feel guilt about their location of birth and social status. Instead, team members need to focus on the importance of using their privilege to help bring focus to the important issues of the nation that they visit.

Konbit Director of Operations, Danilo Cyrius, said it this way: "The best advice I can give to anyone who wants to work in Haiti is to listen to Haitians around you. That can sometimes be difficult because many times foreigners come in with their plans and ideas. But, this is important . . . to listen to Haitians means you believe that they know what's best for their communities."

Local Involvement

People local to the area being visited must be asked to actively participate in a short-term trip. That may mean that leaders at all levels of the local mission participate with teams in some way, and it may include local volunteers partnering with teams toward specific goals. In these partnerships, the local people may need to confront ways they have been conditioned to react in a specific subservient way towards foreigners. Many of our staff and local volunteers at Konbit Haiti work diligently year-round and know that long-term leadership of all nationalities care about their voice, but they still have to overcome this historical pattern of interacting.

Short-term teams need to be willing to step into projects that began with local initiative and will be continued by locals after they leave. For example, Konbit's Water, Sanitation, and Hygiene (WASH) branch conducts water projects in communities all across Haiti. The program is led by five indigenous leaders on staff. Each staff has recruited volunteer teams to help their impact grow in their regions of operation. The program started long before any foreigners were involved, through the innovation and leadership of the Haitian men and women who were dreaming of solutions for their communities and educating themselves the best they could.

A second example of local leadership can be seen in Clelie Cyrius's community center program with Konbit Haiti. A native resident of Konbit's home base, a city called Montrouis, Cyrius took initiative to solve the problems she observed in families in her city. "Children weren't respecting their parents, and parents weren't active in their children's lives," she noted. As a local, she was able to see root causes and culturally appropriate solutions. As Konbit's Family Services Director, Cyrius used a community-center model focused on equipping mothers by offering them practical resources and emotional support. The mothers reported feeling encouraged and even mothered themselves by Cyrius.

Local involvement puts Haitians back in the center of the story, which increases long-term investment in projects and develops the resilience of Haitian leadership. There is a big difference when a person comes to build something with a Haitian person versus doing something for a Haitian person. When Haitians are invited along in a process, Haitians, as well as foreign team members, are able to collaborate, and to take their rightful places in the story of missions.

Literally Standing in the Back

While pre-trip training is essential, we find that it is not sufficient to ensure a copowering mission experience. Short-term team members can read all the books and manuals they are assigned; they can watch documentaries and learn the culture; they can say they are aware of the issues that short-term teams make, and still not hold themselves accountable once their feet hit the foreign soil. This phenomenon highlights the disparity between education and experience, especially when a person is being asked to change a pattern of behavior that is as entrenched as privilege can be.

Thus, we circle back to the importance of practicing "standing in the back" literally, not just figuratively. Moving the body from its usually privileged position to a different physical space consistently reminds the heart, mind and soul to be humble. Placing oneself in a humble location produces a deeper learning than head knowledge alone. Throughout each vision trip, there has to be a level of personal accountability for each team member, and it has to be ongoing. The more team members can keep each other accountable for an attitude of humility, the more successful their experience will be.

An Example of Standing in the Back

To understand the positive impact of a standing-in-the-back approach, consider the following example of a short-term medical mission undertaken in partnership with local Haitians. On this occasion, a team of three medical professionals prepared for their trip by speaking regularly with the cultural broker from Konbit Haiti. The cultural broker was responsible for making sure all parties agreed to the style, dates, and programming of the trip.

Because of their conversations with the cultural broker, the medical professionals were able to target programming to the needs that the community in Haiti had already expressed. First, the medical professionals hosted a three-day long health-education forum for Haitian parents. Topics that locals had asked about were addressed, such as wound-care and how lactating mothers could increase breastmilk production. In the forum, Haitian community members shared their experiences and expertise alongside the medical professionals. This partnership between locals and medical professionals created a mutually beneficial experience by filling in the gaps for the parents who wanted to understand more without creating the perception that western medicine was being preached.

Then, the participants from the health-education forum volunteered alongside the medical professionals at a two-day clinic in the mountains behind the community. This partnership multiplied the impact and effectiveness of the medical professionals' efforts. The local volunteers were able to teach patients as they waited in line for the clinic, and they were able to provide a post-visit follow up for practical, culturally appropriate ways patients could improve their health.

This approach to short-term missions required more communication and coordination than a traditional trip. The medical professionals took a humble posture, understanding that the local teams were the main actors in the drama of Haitian missions, and holding loosely any belief they may have had about the cultural superiority of western medicine. The extra effort in planning, agreeing on expectations, raising up local volunteers, and taking a stand-in-the-back posture was worth it. The local Haitian volunteers and the medical professionals walked away saying the same thing: "I've never experienced something like this."

Mutually Beneficial Impacts

The stand-in-the-back approach benefits both short-term teams and local communities. It gives short-term missionaries an unexpected gift of humility that will serve them in all their future contexts. The short-term team members walk away knowing they have contributed to a system that creates autonomy, resilience, and sustainable transformation. The host country benefits as well, with their story becoming central to their own community's transformation, as it should be. This model has long-term impacts on younger generations, who become prepared to lead as they see models of local leadership. As one of our staff members, Misderline Saint-Armand de Sou-boy said, there is a copowering exchange of information in the Konbit Haiti approach that helps younger generations "feel like [they] can do anything." The future of missions in Haiti belongs to the Haitian people, and we at Konbit Haiti welcome you, as our guest, to play your rightful part in our story.

Clelie Cyrius

Clelie Eugene Cyrius works with Konbit Haiti as a leader of multiple programs. Using her degree in elementary education, she works with over two hundred families in her native, Montrouis, Haiti. She is married and has one son, Samy. She is passionate about Jesus, children, and being a leader.

Danilo Cyrius

Danilo Cyrius was born to help communities create more autonomy in their lives. He is the current Director of Operations for Konbit Haiti and oversees a staff of fifty development practitioners and ministry leaders. He has a big heart for creating sustainable change in his home country, changing the narrative about Haitians, and supporting grassroots development. He uses his education and experience as a missionary on the island of Hispaniola to draw people in, minister to families in crisis, and encourage those recovering from disasters. He is married to Clelie, and they have one child.

Stephanie Robinson

Stephanie Robinson is one of the co-founders of Konbit Haiti and currently serves as the Director of Research and Development for the organization. She's worked in Haiti for ten years and within that time earned a master's of International Community Development. She and her husband split their time between Haiti and the USA. She enjoys being on the water, reading, and spending time with friends.

David Sanon

David Sanon has been a community development practitioner for fifteen years. He has overseen multiple areas of water, sanitation, and hygiene projects and teachings in addition to helping local communities protect their water resources. As a development missionary, he has worked in both Haiti and its neighbor, the Dominican Republic. He is originally from Montrouis, Haiti, and has worked with the WASH (water, sanitation, and hygiene) programs with Konbit Haiti since its inception. He is on the leadership team for Konbit Haiti and works hard to make sure people have access to clean drinking water and training. He and his wife have been together for over a decade and have two children.

Andrea Sielaff

Andrea Sielaff works with The Seattle School of Theology and Psychology as a Researcher for Resilient Leaders Project and as adjunct faculty teaching Vocational Direction. In addition, she leads apprenticeship groups for M.Div students at Fuller Seminary. She was previously in campus ministry with InterVarsity Christian Fellowship, going on to earn a masters degree in Counseling from Northern Arizona University.

6

When NonBelievers Go on Mission Trips[1]

CJ Quartlbaum *with* Crystal Kupper

Legendary UCLA basketball coach John Wooden once said, "Sports doesn't build character, it reveals it." When it comes to seeing the truth about a person's heart, the same can be said of mission trips.

Not long ago, I worked for a short-term missions organization in one of the largest cities in the country—one in which I continue to invest as a consultant. We essentially provide existing ministries with a volunteer base during the summer. We partner with soup kitchens, shelters, storehouses, churches, community gardens and more. The volunteers tend to be groups of students, families, churches, and organizations from across the country with a desire to serve in the inner city. They are mostly suburban and affluent.

Many who come on our trips are believers with genuine hearts to serve the city. Unfortunately, this is not the case for everyone and in my experience, it is common to have more nonbelievers on a trip than you would think. We don't require that people be believers in order to do a mission

---

1. Portions of this essay appeared in *The Witness*, https://thewitnessbcc.com.

trip with us, but everyone knows who we are and what we are about, and thus know what they are signing up for.

It is rare that we receive outright atheists, but "nonbelief" takes different forms. There are the people who simply come because it will get them school credit and be a good resume booster. Others just want a cool, decently affordable trip to New York City—and serving for a few hours a day is simply the price they have to pay. *Then there are those who grew up in church and are steeped in church culture.* They have spent their entire lives doing churchy things but seem to have had no true transforming experience with the Lord.

Consequently, many of the short-term visitors I've worked with come with minds that are closed to the beauty that can be seen in difference, and attitudes that are ungracious towards others who are not like them. In my experience with STM groups, I have come to recognize some of the more common biases that short-termers carry with them. Prevalent among them is bias against urban contexts in general, stereotypes about poor people, and prejudice based on race and ethnicity. And the more I see of these signs of nonbelief, the more I am convinced that what short-term missionaries need to seek *before* they come to the city is "to be transformed by the renewing of [their] minds" as Paul put it—and to seek a real, transformative belief in the gospel that they ostensibly come to give witness to.[2]

The Demonized City

Most of our groups are from upper middle class, suburban, majority white churches. These groups have limited exposure to the city. Most of what they know about New York City they have learned through television and movies. And cable news reminds them regularly that the city is a big, scary place, full of dangerous people.

When it comes to urban mission opportunities, many choose New York because the city represents what they perceive as a worst-case example of all that is wrong with big cities in general. So many of the visiting groups hold an overly simple caricature of New York that makes the trip simultaneously terrifying yet thrilling. They come then to minister to the hordes of poor people living in destitution. Many seek prayer support for their trip, because *as everyone knows*, New York is a god-forsaken city, overrun by Jesus-hating liberals and steeped in sin.

2. Rom 12:2 (NIV).

At the end of a team's visit, I would always ask the departing students if there were any major misconceptions that had been broken over the course of their New York experience. Usually, I got some version of the answer: "I'm surprised by the number of churches here. I thought New York was a godless city." To a certain extent, I can't blame them. We have an entire generation of church planters who have moved here to "save the city." In garnering support from their suburban home churches, a good number of them I am sure paint a compelling vision of the city as a barren wasteland of heathens needing to be saved. STM teams often use the same strategy of course. The depiction of the city in such negative terms—dangerous to all but the bravest of missionaries (short-term OR long-term), is one of those "imaginaries" of missions that Brian Howell insists we must change—enduring illusions that keep us from seeing what is real and true in a given context.[3] To that end, in my debriefing with the teams I always pointed out the fact that there are over six thousand churches in the city—and plenty of them are doing the long-term, systemic, incarnational work of serving the poor and marginalized that, unlike the work of short-term teams, actually makes for real, lasting change and authentic witness. If that is any indicator, this is no godless place.

The Undeserving Poor

Sadly, when it comes to perceptions of the poor, many of the churches that send teams to us tend to be the "pull yourself up by your bootstraps" type with the "we worked hard and you should too" mindset. The teams they send are sincere in their desire to help—yet they do so with the simplistic assumption that poor people are where they are because of the choices they've made. There is no framework for taking into account the effects of years of systemic oppression, the struggles of being the only breadwinner and losing your job, or having a crippling illness change everything for your family. Everyone is surprised to learn the average age of a homeless person in New York City is just nine years old. No matter what your ideology, you can't blame a nine-year-old for being poor.

The persistent judgements that so many of our STM visitors bring with them stand in stark contrast to the grace and compassion that characterized Jesus' life. The values framework by which they try to make sense of the poor seems to have less to do with the bibles they carry, and more to do

3. See Brian Howell's observations in chapter 13 of this volume, 147–161.

with the capitalist system that makes sense to white middle class suburbanites who benefit from it.

In fact, the system doesn't offer many benefits to those who are already poor—as Jesus knew well. Yet this is difficult for the mostly middle class STM visitors to understand, and as a result their attempts to offer any kind of relevant or relatable witness are hindered. Looking back, I am one of those they would come to "save." I was (still am) one of the broken and needy in the city. If I were to come across some of these STM groups back then, I would have wanted nothing to do with their Jesus. My poor, immigrant, hard-working, black family would be appalled and offended by the ideologies and rhetoric that's often spouted about our laziness and our need to "get it together."

The Incomprehensible "Other"

I have learned from painful experience that the most destructive sorts of illusions that white, suburban short-termers bring with them stem from ingrained prejudices based on a person's race or ethnicity. When such attitudes go unexamined, not only do STM visitors have no meaningful witness in the city—they actually end up dehumanizing those they come to serve in profoundly un-Christlike ways.

One of the unique things our organization does during mission trips is something we call "prayer tours." We walk through different neighborhoods in different boroughs, highlighting connections to historical events and current issues in ways that are meant to help the teams to pray for these communities. This past year, we added a stop that offered the opportunity to learn about the Black Lives Matter movement. However, our explanations of the need for racial justice and reconciliation in our city do not always go well. Here are typical responses we receive:

- "Isn't the problem that black people are insubordinate and just need to listen to authority?"
- "We felt as though Black Lives Matter was being pushed on us." (This is in response to our closing words: "You can stand by and let these injustices continue to happen or you can do something.")

I wish our problems with racial insensitivity ended there. In one instance, a group leader from the deep south had to be asked to stop using the N-word. In another, one of the girls on a team cried for three hours because she didn't feel safe in our neighborhood—and although she couldn't quite put her finger on it, the place just felt "sketch" and made her nervous. And on another occasion a team leader, referring to black people, complained that she just didn't know how to speak to "them" sometimes. Honestly, it was exhausting.

Once we had a group of students carve their phone numbers into a table with the message: "Call us, we're white." I suppose it is possible that the young people who had cut those words into the table might have rationalized their vandalism as a covert way to offer a rescue rope. Nevertheless, their actions indicated that on some deep level these were people whose hearts hadn't yet been transformed by the power of the gospel. In that sense they were "nonbelievers"—and that made them, from a missions perspective, unqualified and unable to offer any sort of meaningful witness.

In Need of a Savior

When my organization hosts STM teams, we do as much as we can to deconstruct some of the misconceptions and dishonoring beliefs that some team members might be carrying with them. In so doing, we understand that ultimately the only way that hearts are changed is through the work of the Spirit. At best, we can only help them to understand the ways they need to change, and provide a context for what is essentially a kind of conversion. On the first night that groups arrive, our city hosts walk them through a review of basic gospel principles, helping to make direct connections to the realities of the urban context. During the week, we structure the prayer tours to remind people repeatedly about the transforming work of Jesus and the cross. And at the end of each week, we hold a worship night where we reiterate lessons that again place the focus on our hope in Christ's redeeming power.

In our best weeks, we've seen clear examples of STM participants who have acknowledged their biases and had their hearts and minds renewed. In so many words, they'll tell us: "I was blind but now I see." They not only take with them the truths they've learned to share with their home community; some even commit to returning to serve in the city long term.

More often, though, our efforts haven't had such impact—and that has everything to do with a lack of soul-level preparatory work that really should have happened long before they came to "save" our city. Most come with that outward-facing savior stance that works against the *inward* gaze that personal transformation requires.

My years of experience working with STMs have convinced me that, as long as short-term visitors hold on to the illusion that their only purpose is to bless others with their brief presence in the city, this "savior mentality" only serves to insulate them from seeing the ways in which they themselves are needy. And when they are blinded by biases about urban communities or jaded by stereotypes of poor, there is no room for understanding the complexities of the problems of the city or the solutions that actually might make a difference.

Ethical Photography on Short-Term Trips

RACHEL NESBITT

WHEN THINKING ABOUT ETHICAL photography, the question is simple: how can we use photography to provide dignity and respect to those all around the world? The answer is also simple: we must see people through the eyes of Jesus *before* we see them through the lens of a camera.

There are many issues with the way that photography is handled during short-term trips. In the worst cases, visitors in a community take manipulative photos of their trip in order to evoke emotional responses, gain funding, or receive more "likes" on social media. However, even those with the best intentions tend to take photos without considering the people they are photographing. When we take a photograph, what is our purpose? Are we seeing the person as God sees them or simply taking a photo to shock our friends back home or document our trip? We dishonor people when we flippantly take their photo without first taking a posture of humility and asking permission.

God made every single person unique, weaving them lovingly together, like a work of art. Christians believe that every single human being bears the image of God (*imago Dei*), that each person is fearfully and wonderfully made[4]. Slowing down and considering how our pictures appear to those we are photographing allow us the chance to look past appearance and truly see another person. At first, we begin to see the unique physical attributes they have, how they move and what they look like. But when we really look into the eyes of another image bearer, we begin to see beyond the physical. *This person is a living, breathing person just like me. They feel pain, sorrow, anger and joy just like me.* To contemplate something, as the Jesuit priest Walter Burghardt famously put it, is to take "a long, loving look at the real."[5] When we can step back and really contemplate who we are seeing, awe and wonder enables us to treat people with the utmost care, deep love, and reverence. When this happens, we get a glimpse of how God sees every person and the value he has for each one.

Photography is a powerful tool that can be used for lasting change in the world, starting with the person looking through the lens of a camera. As a culture that is conditioned for instant gratification and cameras attached to our back pockets at all times, we *must* learn to slow down. This slowing down before taking a photograph is an exercise in humility, allowing us to really see the people we are photographing as we learn part of their stories. We must approach STM trips with the mindset that the local people are the experts, and we must value them as God does—with humility and a heart that sees and values His creation. When we have this as our foundation, our photographs can be used to bring honor to those we serve, to work toward lasting social change, and to help bring God's kingdom to earth.

Practical Considerations when Photographing on STMs:

1. Serve under the guidance of an organization who has a known presence in the community and has already built

---

4. Psalm 139:14 (NIV).
5. Ambrosino, *"Smartphones and our memories."*

relationships with local people. Then, *ask* these trusted cultural guides about how photography may be reacted to in their culture. Lastly, respect the decision of your host and humbly accept whatever conclusion they come to regarding photographs of their community and ministry.

2. Always ask permission when you are taking photos of people. The term "taking photographs" is illuminating in the context of STMs. It is, quite literally, *taking* something from someone—someone we have come to serve. Photographs should not be "taken"; they should be "given"[6]. It's vital to ask permission prior to photographing and equally important before posting it to any type of social media. If permission is not asked, it can be assumed that the photographer thinks they have a right to *take* a photograph from the person(s), an attitude which goes against the very purpose of an STM trip. I think of my own daughter who is one year old. I am responsible to protect her vulnerability and censor who takes photographs of her, as well as what is shared outside of our family. I would expect someone to ask before taking a photo of my daughter, and then respect whatever response I give them. We should offer the same respect to those we meet on our trips.

3. Seek to show the dignity, resilience, and respect in the individuals and communities where you are taking photos. For example, we can use our camera to highlight the amazing creative ways that people economically provide for their families. We can highlight the strength of women who carry hundreds of pounds of bricks on their heads to bring home money for their families. Or capture how children make toys from what we might consider trash. We can document the pride that a family has in its meager living space and the way they survive and thrive with less. We can snap a photo of the smiles of children demonstrating the way they write their letters or depict how a local clinic goes to slums and assists its people. Record things that bring hope and show resilience.

6. Bogre, *Photography as Activism*, 64.

Our purpose should always be to lift people up in our photographs and highlight their value.

4. Be aware of the danger of "poverty porn."

> [Poverty porn is] any type of media, be it written, photographed or filmed, which exploits the poor's condition in order to generate the necessary sympathy for selling newspapers or increasing charitable donations or support a given cause . . . The subjects are overwhelmingly children, with the material usually characterized by images or descriptions of suffering, malnourished or otherwise helpless persons.[7]

These images evoke strong emotions, producing shock and moving people to donate to a cause. However, many times these photos are not representative of the person's actual situation and do not show the resilience of the person or people group. Often, money is being raised at the expense of a person (often a child) being depicted as helpless, which is hardly ever the case. Engaging in poverty porn is the opposite of treating hosts with respect and dignity.

5. Consider asking your host to oversee taking photos of their community. We can humbly choose to put a camera in the hands of the host culture to represent their own lives. Perhaps the best way to represent a people group is when a host culture can represent themselves in their own creative way.

Hopefully these practical suggestions are just the beginning as we continue to humbly evaluate our use of photography on STMs. Remember to slow down, *look* at people the way Jesus looks at you, and be willing to reframe how photos are captured on your STM.

Rachel Nesbitt

Rachel Nesbitt has a master's degree from Northwest University in International Community Development and a bachelor of arts

---

7. Collin, "What is 'poverty porn,'" https://www.etio.ca/post/2020/06/01/poverty-porn-and-covid-19.

in Sociology from Seattle Pacific University. She has a passion for photography and has captured images from many nations including India, a place she has a deep love for and connection to. She has used photography as a means to raise money for ministries in the south of India and simply takes photos as a hobby. She currently resides in Ellensburg, Washington, with her husband. Together, they have two baby girls. They are her full-time job and her current photo subjects.

Bibliography

Ambrosino, Brandon. "Smartphones and Our Memories: Don't Take a Picture. It'll Last Longer." *The Globe and Mail* (2018).

Collin, M. "What is 'Poverty Porn' and Why Does it Matter for Development?" *Aid Thoughts* (2009).

Michelle Bogre, *Photography as Activism: Images for Social Change*. New York: Focal, 2012.

Homework and Heart-Work

For these reasons I would argue that, if any church endeavors to send short-term missionaries for the sake of the gospel, they need to make sure that the ones who are sent actually *believe* in the gospel to the point where their hearts and minds have been transformed—or at least be aware of and open to the continual process of transformation that leads us ever closer to Christ-likeness. Only then will they be able to offer any sort of compelling witness to God's work in their lives. In preparation for urban missions, those who would be part of the team need to do the necessary heart-work that seeks to identify and address the unhelpful beliefs and assumptions that, if left in the dark, will always keep people from being agents of God's grace in the city.

Importantly, churches that truly seek a transformation of perspective don't need to figure it all out on their own, in isolation from the context where they want to serve. Before any suburban congregation hops on the plane to LaGuardia to just "help out however they can," it would do well to consider forming a partnership between their members and those of the place they hope to serve. In a city like New York, with thousands of existent churches, what would it look like for a church from Ohio to partner with one in the city in advance of their trip?

The months preceding an STM trip could be spent getting to get to know people's names and hearing their stories. Actual friendships—not just mere run-ins that come and go with seven days of service—can develop this way, creating the possibility for members of both communities to stay in touch after the trip. Long-term partnerships for short-term missions lend themselves to the continuation of consistent service in subsequent years as well. True investment in a place goes beyond the week-long drop-in visit. Rather, true investment means taking the time to become intimately aware of the causes of suffering among the people you are seeking to love.

What it also means, though, is allowing the ones you intend to serve to see into the needs of your community as well, and to be humble enough to allow them to love and serve you. Partnerships thus make possible the practice of "reverse mission trips," whereby sending churches become receiving churches first. Suburban and rural areas face their own versions of brokenness; and people *everywhere* need Jesus. Furthermore, reverse mission trips help to transform the hierarchical savior narrative. Only when those who are used to "saving" begin to understand their own need for a savior can true heart transformation begin. Only when engagement happens with those who are objectified as "other," can stereotypes about the city, about the poor, and even about people of color be questioned and deconstructed. And only when there are honest conversations with those who have been the objects of prejudice can repentance and restoration of relationship begin.

I have become convinced that the process of preparation for a STM trip should always include the sort of honest soul searching that begins with the following assumptions:

- Like everyone, I do have biases that I cannot fully see and acknowledge.

- I will, with the help of my teammates and leaders, seek to identify these prior to and during the trip.

- I will also expect that my experiences in the city may bring to the surface new awareness of false and damaging assumptions.

- I will practice humility that opens my heart and mind to learning from the people that I encounter on the trip.

- As a STM team we commit to helping one another to see truth, seek healing, and practice repentance when faced with these hard truths about ourselves—all for the sake of becoming more like Christ.

If prospective team members can't assume the humility and teachability implicit in these statements (or something along these lines), they probably ought not to go. As I see it, this is one crucial way we need to think differently if there is any hope for changing the broken aspects of urban short-term missions.

It might seem to some that, if renewed and renewable minds are prerequisite for urban short-term missions, that might be setting the bar too high. Might these higher standards result in fewer STM teams doing urban missions? Frankly, I hope so. Sending unprepared teams can be a sad misuse of resources, and it usually does little if any good for urban communities. Still, as a believer in Christ, I am never without hope. If sending churches can help the people they send to transform their hearts and minds well in advance of a trip, then the practices of STMs might just be radically reformed enough that they produce deep and lasting good for everyone involved.

Claude Quartlbaum

CJ Quartlbaum is a writer and speaker from Brooklyn, NY. He is the creator of Live & Labor, the platform he uses to equip the church with simple teachings on living in the way of Jesus. He is a father of three and loves basketball, food, and reading about the most random things. You can follow him on the socials @CJ_Quartlbaum.

Crystal Kupper

Crystal Kupper is a journalist, marathon runner, mother and military wife currently stationed in Arizona. Thus far, she and her husband have parented seven children from four countries who arrived via birth, adoption, foreign exchange or informal foster care. Having lived in Europe and traveled to dozens of countries, she is passionate about orphan justice, family preservation, and deinstitutionalization, especially for children with disabilities. Her writing frequently touches on international community development issues and themes.

7

The Economy of Exploitation

Gloria Kennedy and Buken Onyango,
with Jeremy Cook *and* Andrea Sielaff

In the year 2016, over 1.6 million American Christians ventured on short-term missions, spending a staggering $2.4 billion.[1] On the one hand this evidence of generosity is fantastic news because it means American Christians are taking Jesus's exhortation of feeding the hungry, clothing the naked, and healing the sick seriously.[2] But a closer look at the long-term impact of these short-term trips reveals the disturbing truth that sometimes the best intentions lead to unintended harm. Well-meaning STMs are not helping kids in Kenya; instead, they are actually creating the conditions for children to be exploited for economic gain.

In this essay, we will address the unintended consequences of STM visits to orphanages and children's homes in Kenya. We will also exhort the western church to face the truth of what their actions are really doing to Kenyan society. Though STM teams seem to be motivated by love, often their desire for significance is warping that love into harm. Real love requires

1. Bartelme, "Do No Harm?"
2. Matt 25:35–40 (NIV).

looking beyond the church's desire to serve in self-important ways, and to ask instead what the real needs are. To that end, this chapter will also offer a revisioning of what the global church can actually do to care for these children through listening to and partnering with what the people of Kenya are already doing. (From this point on, the term Residential Care Institutions—RCIs—will be used instead of orphanage, because the majority of children in these institutions are not actually orphans.)

We begin with this assumption: churches want what is best for kids, both the kids in their own community and kids around the world. Western churches often send STMs to RCIs in obedience to James 1:27, which encourages Christians "to look after orphans and widows in their distress."[3] A majority of STM participants are young adults sent by the church with the intention of exposing them to the realities of other cultures, spreading the gospel, and engaging with the children in the RCIs.[4] The STM participants aim to provide for the emotional and material needs of the children, such as companionship, conversation, toys, and household amenities. These good intentions, however, do not reflect the actual results of STMs visiting RCIs in Kenya. The terrible truth is that—while STM participants view visiting RCIs as an opportunity to serve the poor, obey biblical exhortations about orphans, and spread the gospel—recruiters, traffickers, and the corrupt heads of some of these institutions view these vulnerable children as a lucrative way to make money.[5]

As unscrupulous institutions are established and visited by STM teams, children are harmed by poor living conditions, disrupted schooling, and attachment issues. Some of the children in these institutions are even victims of child trafficking. Because harms caused by living in an institution can be pervasive and long-lasting, institutionalization should always be a last resort. Kinship care is a far healthier environment for children. As Andrea Freidus, a western researcher on the African context, argues,

3. James 1:27 (NIV).

4. Anonymous #1. Personal interview. 26 June 2020.

5. A note on sources: In addition to news articles and research, sources for this chapter include first-hand accounts of RCI experiences. One of the authors, Buken Onyango, has worked with RCIs for over a decade as a volunteer and a teaching assistant. Some of the people who agreed to be interviewed requested to remain anonymous: a number of them either work for the RCIs they once lived in or have family members who are somehow benefiting from the RCIs, and they fear repercussions from RCI directors. Nevertheless, they were compelled to share the truth with us because they wanted you to hear the stories that they have never been allowed to tell.

[Orphans] are just not abandoned in the way people in the West think. If there are family networks that these children are willing to go to, then why institutionalize them? We don't do that in the U.S. anymore, and most [western] European countries don't do it anymore, because we know it's bad for kids.[6]

The good news is that the government in Kenya, along with several Kenyan organizations, are working to end these abuses and return children to kinship care. For those who have a heart for the children currently residing in RCIs, the best way to help is to invest in organizations that focus on family reunification and strengthening. The western church has a significant part to play in making this change happen. When the western church understands what is really happening in RCIs, it should prompt soul-searching about why churches choose to serve in self-important ways. As churches see their mixed motives and send fewer STMs, there will be less demand for RCIs. Less demand for RCIs will result in less exploitation of vulnerable children.

For these efforts and other ministry partnerships to be truly effective, however, the western church will have to listen to the Kenyan church as its equal. This requires awareness of how power dynamics based on economic disparities have eroded partnerships in the global church. Because of these power dynamics, the western church must actively humble itself and listen before asserting its own solutions; only then will good intentions actually bear good fruit.

Supply and Demand: The Economy of Residential Childcare Institutions

There is an irresistible power in the way that vulnerable children tug at the heartstrings: sad eyes, the threat of hunger, the irony of innocence lost by the most innocent of all. This emotional response to suffering children is right and good. It compels Christians to action to protect and nurture those who cannot protect themselves. Out of these good intentions, the short-term mission trip to an orphanage has become a rite of passage in many western churches. However, these sincere intentions to help have led to a commodification of Kenyan children as the economics of supply and demand make running a Residential Care Institution a profitable venture.

---

6. Lu, "Why There's A Global Outcry."

In 2018 it was estimated that around forty-two thousand children lived in 854 RCIs across Kenya.[7] But over 80% of children in Kenyan RCIs labelled as "orphans" have at least one living parent.[8] Michelle Oliel is a co-founder of Stahili Foundation, an organization dedicated to shutting down Kenyan orphanages by reuniting children with their families. Her experience reveals that

> . . . the children are being commodified and placed in an orphan-
> age for the sole purpose of bringing in donations and other various
> donated goods. And this is done intentionally. It's not an accident.
> It's not an accident that in most of the cases that [the Stahili Foun-
> dation has] dealt with, children have families. They are exploiting
> vulnerable children, vulnerable people, vulnerable guardians.[9]

RCIs "largely [feed] off the effects of poverty, lack of access to services and education, disability and family breakdown."[10] Profit-minded RCI directors reach out to middlemen to recruit "orphans." These recruiters approach an impoverished parent, grandparent, or close relative, convincing them that giving up their kin to an RCI will mean access to a better life, food, clothing, shelter, and most of all an education. One such case is Regina Weveti, who reluctantly sent her niece, Teresia Wairimu, to an orphanage. Weveti recalls, "I wanted Teresia to stay with me like a daughter, but I didn't have enough money. When I was approached by someone who could take her into an orphanage, I didn't have a choice." However, "food, education, and safety proved to be a false promise for Teresia . . . the orphanage director ensured that the lives of the orphans revolved around foreign volunteers who traveled specifically to help children." In contrast to what the recruiters told her aunt, Teresia went hungry when RCI directors withheld food, missed school to entertain foreign volunteers, and had her physical and emotional safety compromised by RCI staff.[11]

In some cases, demand for "orphans" results in child trafficking. This happens when recruiters don't consult the family of the child. Instead, they resort to stealing and kidnapping them from slums, bus stations, hospitals, and even churches. The recruiters's motivation is simple: getting paid fifty to one-hundred dollars for each child they place at the RCI. Farai Sevenzo,

7. Mwangi, "Programme to De-Institutionalize."

8. Global Affairs Canada, *Taking Child Protection*, 8.

9. CNN, "Orphanage 'Recruited Kids to Get Donations."

10. Sloth-Nielsen, "Kenya Takes Next Steps."

11. CNN, "Orphanage 'Recruited Kids to Get Donations."'

CNN's Nairobi correspondent stated, "Not all orphanages are corrupt or guilty of trafficking. Still the UN and other groups are now warning about child trafficking to orphanages around the world."[12]

While walking around the neighborhood of Kibra, Onyango, one of this essay's authors, came across a woman who knew his connections to RCIs. She pulled out a picture of her daughter and asked whether he had seen her. Onyango said he had not. She then relayed that a recruiter had approached her promising to take her daughter shopping for a school uniform and to return her in two days's time so the mother could escort her to boarding school. That was two years ago, and the mother has not seen the recruiter or her daughter since.

Dr. Krish Kandidah, founding director of Home for Good, a United Kingdom-based charity focused on transitioning children from RCIs into loving homes, explained, "The money and support that westerners give may be 'unwittingly fueling the orphanage system' . . . Many of these orphanages are kept open by the support and demand of international volunteers."[13] In order to get STMs to visit their RCIs, many Kenyan RCI directors market their homes as the best option for vulnerable children. Some of the children are told to share heartbreaking stories, but are strictly coached on what to say, including only the details that will tug at the hearts and the wallets of well-intentioned Christians, who respond by sending STMs and donations. To be clear, we are not saying that only STMs and the western church are responsible for driving the demand of RCIs; other volunteers play a role, too. Nevertheless, creating demand for these trips implicates STMs in the harm that happens to children because of these RCIs.

Unintended Consequences: How Residential Care Institutions Harm Children

While STM teams may have a great experience visiting a Residential Care Institution, they should be aware that what they witness during their visits may not match the reality of the children's lives when they are not around. RCI hosts in Kenya often create a carefully staged illusion for the seven to ten days that the STM visits. The RCIs hope STM teams will think that the children are well cared for, and thus trust the organization with more

12. CNN, "Orphanage 'Recruited Kids to Get Donations.'"

13. Mbakwe, "Christians Urged to Stop Volunteering," www.youtube.com/watch?v=8xwQXXcvzjg.

donations. Unfortunately, when an STM team is not around, the children are often receiving a totally different, sub-standard level of care.

Creating this illusion of a well-run RCI involves a ramping-up and ramping-down process. Here is the ramp-up process that a typical RCI does in the two weeks prior to a STM visit: The children—who are usually dressed in tattered clothes and broken shoes, if they are wearing any—are given a new wardrobe to wear just for the days when the STM teams visit. Their usual bed sheets are changed to special "STM" bedding. The daily casual wipe down of their dorms is replaced with a stricter, more rigorous cleaning. Thus, the stage is set and the illusion is played out for the STM team. When the STM participants leave, the ramp-down begins. The special STM bed sheets, clothes and shoes are taken away and replaced with the previous ones. Toys and gifts are either locked up or sold by the RCI directors. The usual RCI program resumes with its sub-standard level of care until another STM comes along. As would be expected, these losses are experienced as a kind of trauma by the children, some of whom express their hurt through crying fits or a refusal to eat.

Education is another area that is negatively impacted by STM teams. When STM teams visit, RCI-funded schools cancel their regular curriculum to cater to the teams. This impacts not only the "orphans" who live at the institution, but also other local children who depend on that school for their education. Even when an RCI doesn't have an associated school, the children who live there can fall behind in their schoolwork when a team comes to visit. These children may still go to school during the day, but when they return to the RCI after school they are expected to engage with the STM team. Kamau, who resided in an RCI, stated that "[it was] challenging to learn to adjust from time to time with [the guests] presence as the timetable changes to favor them. Our schoolwork [was] affected, as by the time we are free with them we [were] already tired and ready to sleep without doing our homework assigned in school."[14] Based on Onyango's experience, as well as that of his colleagues who also worked in RCIs, it was common for students to have multiple STMs visit them annually. If a child's education is interrupted six or seven times during the year for three weeks at a time, it is difficult to catch up and remain competitive.

Residential Care Institutions can also cause deeper emotional harm as well as physical or sexual abuse. Peter Kamau Muthui provides evidence of the emotional harm that comes from neglect in RCIs. In the institution

14. Kamau, personal interview, 28 October 2020.

Muthui grew up in, they had only two housemothers who took turns taking care of the thirty children. He shared that the children never wanted for material things, but because of this neglect, they struggled to feel loved or form any attachment.[15] Joseph Mwuara, a twenty-year-old trafficking survivor, experienced exploitation and witnessed physical abuse at a Kenyan RCI: "It was terrible. We had to do a lot of work to get food. If we failed, we were denied food as punishment. They used a lot of physical violence. They beat one boy and broke his leg."[16] According to child-advocacy groups Forget Me Not and Lumos, "Placing a child in an orphanage quadruples the risk of sexual violence."[17] Sadly, this sexual abuse is sometimes a result of RCIs opening their doors to STMs, who may unwittingly include child predators in their groups.

Another significant harm that children face when growing up in an institution is disruption to their ability to form attachments. Attachment—the ability to have lasting, healthy relationships—is key to emotional regulation, resilience, and success as an adult. As is the case with Muthui's experience, RCIs often lack enough consistent caregivers for children to receive attention and form bonds. STM participants also disrupt the children's ability to attach; participants enter the children's lives for a brief but intense time and then leave. Stephen Ucembe, Founder of Kenya Society of Careleavers, experienced this firsthand as a child. He recounted, "We did indeed cling to their presence like they were never going to leave; but eventually, they had to leave. Deep inside they had shattered our trust."[18]

It seems almost impossible for these children to thrive emotionally as adults when their childhood years were characterized by broken relationships. In fact, the global consensus among decades of studies is that it's common for children who grew up in RCIs to experience troubled adulthoods. According to 2006 UNICEF report which cited a study in Russia, "one in three young people who leave residential institutions becomes homeless, one in five ends up with a criminal record, and one in ten commits suicide."[19] Muthui recounted the following about his struggles to reintegrate into society after growing up in an RCI:

15. Muthui, "Interview: My Childhood," 8–9.
16. Batha, "Calls Mount to Stop Orphanages Exploiting."
17. Batha, "Factbox: Most Children."
18. Faith to Action Initiative, *Short-Term Missions: Guidance to Support.*
19 Lu,"Why There's A Global Outcry."

I was ill-prepared for life outside the home. Like many who had gone before me, I was left to manage alone. I had spent years following a structured routine where I had little or no choice, and so I struggled with independent life. Forming relationships, cooking and budgeting were challenging for me. The lack of positive interaction with adults at the children's home meant I lacked personal confidence and key social skills. This included the skills necessary for starting a family.[20]

Lacking life skills, social support, and the ability to form healthy attachments, children who grow up in an RCI are vulnerable to human trafficking. According to the United States Department of State's Office to Monitor and Combat Trafficking in Persons:

> Even when a child leaves or ages out of a residential institution, the vulnerability to human trafficking continues, in part due to the physical and psychological damage many of these children have suffered. The societal isolation of residential institutions often prevents children from building stable, long-term familial or social relationships. By depriving children of opportunities to develop a social support network, receive adequate schooling, experience common life or social situations, and practice using cognitive reasoning and problem-solving skills, residential institutions leave those departing from institutional care more vulnerable to traffickers' schemes. Some traffickers, in recognizing the heightened vulnerability of these children, wait for and target those who leave or age out of institutions.[21]

Sending churches and nonprofits are asked to deeply consider the life-long, pervasive harm that is caused by their demand to send short-term missions teams.

Given all the harm caused by RCIs, it should be noted that institutionalization is not the only option for providing care to vulnerable children. As noted above, most children in RCIs have a living parent. Sadly, as long as RCIs continue to exist, some parents will consider them as better options for their child than their own home. Listening to former residents of RCIs reveals that is often not the case. One of these individuals, who preferred to remain anonymous, recalled:

---

20. Muthui, "Interview: My Childhood," 8–9.
21. United States Department of State, *Civilian Security.*

I am twenty-three years old now, and I was in the orphanage for six to seven years of my life. It was one of the hardest experiences I have ever encountered in my entire life. One morning after Christmas celebrations my mom told me that my aunt was coming for me to go and stay with her. It never struck my mind that I would be living at her orphanage among forty other children younger and older than me—and that it would become my second home. Shortly after I started living there, I forgot my other siblings. After the seven years, when I returned to living with my mom again, I considered her to be a total stranger. During my entire stay at the orphanage, both my parents were alive, and I believe they could have afforded to pay for my school fees and feed all of us even if the school wouldn't have been as good or the food as plentiful. I never thought I would be separated from my family so suddenly and still feel disconnected from them after I returned.[22]

Each year that a child is separated from his or her biological parent(s), it increasingly weakens the familial bond between them. Seven years of separation made this man's family feel like strangers to him. Clearly, he would have preferred to have attended a school of lower standing if it meant that he could be home with his family.

A Way Forward: Global Partnership for Kinship Care

As Kenyan believers, we exhort our brothers and sisters in the West to rethink their uncritical support of Residential Care Institutions in our country. Instead, they should shift their efforts toward partnering with organizations that prioritize reuniting children with their families and strengthening the family unit. One such organization is Child in Family Focus, which promotes family-based care for orphaned and vulnerable children in Kenya. Founder and former RCI resident P. K. Muthui stated,

> God's plan for caring for children is the family. It is a much better plan than caring for them in children's homes—no matter how beautiful and well run a children's home may be. For those who are supporting children's homes, now is the time for a change of mindset. Challenge those managing orphanages to transform them into community support centres. These centres can strengthen families so they can care for their own children and orphaned relatives. If

22. Anonymous #6, personal interview, 2 Nov. 2020.

kinship care is unavailable or unsuitable, we should support other
forms of alternative care, such as foster care and adoption.[23]

Though their systems are not perfect, many countries in the West have
already changed how it cares for its own vulnerable children; instead of orphanages, children are placed in families through kinship care, foster care,
and adoption. The western church, with its deep commitment to the family
of God, needs to change its mindset and strive to care for children in less
developed countries as they would care for their own.

If the western church can change its mindset from supporting RCIs
to supporting family reunification and kinship care, it would be joining
the ongoing efforts of the Kenyan government, Kenyan locals, the United
Nations, and several charity organizations who are already working to transition children from RCIs to families. In 2014, in response to the deplorable
conditions of twenty-one RCIs and the harmful ways they impact children,
Kenyan President Uhuru Kenyatta issued a ban on the registration of more
RCIs.[24] In 2017 the Kenyan government announced a long term plan to end
the institutionalization of children.[25] In accordance with this plan the Association of Charitable Children Institutions of Kenya (ACCIK) launched
a two-year program in 2018 across seven Kenyan counties, titled, "Protection of Children from Family Separation, Abuse, Neglect and Exploitation
Project." Its purpose is to reunite thousands of children who are currently
residing in RCIs with their families. Stephen Ndung'u, the national chair of
the ACCIK firmly believes that "children's homes should never be permanent living places for vulnerable minors who need a family set up . . . We
want to discourage families from bringing their children to [RCIs]. The
children should be kept close to family members for wholesome growth."[26]

At its core, the argument we are making is not about whether any RCI
directors have good intentions to love the children in their homes. They
very well might. We also acknowledge that there are some RCIs that provide
education, housing, and food to children who would otherwise go without
it. However, the issue remains: if an RCI, however well-intentioned, does
not aim to eventually place children with families, then it is not acting in
the best interest of the children.

23. Muthui, "Interview: My Childhood," 8–9.
24. Budd, Ken. "I Spent Time in a Kenyan Orphanage."
25. Sloth-Nielsen, "Kenya Takes Next Steps."
26. Mwangi, "Programme to De-Institutionalize."

This assessment is shared by James Kassaga Arinaitwe, an Aspen Institute New Voices Fellow and the CEO and co-founder of Teach for Uganda, who was raised by his grandmother after his mother died of cancer and his father of AIDS. Arinaitwe explained, "If you really want to help [children], help their extended families take care of them."[27] The great news is that family-based care, which is the best form of care for these children, is more cost-effective than institutional care. A UNICEF and Government of Kenya Report, "Guidelines for the Alternative Family Care of Children in Kenya," states that "In South Africa, for example, the monthly cost of statutory residential care can be six times more than the cost of providing care to children living in vulnerable families (i.e. home-based care and support for families affected by HIV and AIDS), and four times more expensive than statutory foster care or adoption."[28]

Shifting this mindset in the western church from "orphanage" care to kinship support requires humility: a humility that is aware of the power dynamics that come into play in partnerships with unequal financial resources. A humility that searches the heart for mixed motives. And a humility that is willing to listen instead of assuming. Too often, as ACC International argued,

> Power and privilege can inadvertently create hierarchy in relationships and unintentionally silence the voices of the less powerful party . . . [The suggestions of westerners] are often agreed to—even when they are inappropriate or counterproductive. This results in donor driven programs that are developed in response to donor initiation rather than the community's or children's true needs.[29]

This power differential results in RCI directors not saying anything against STM-proposed programs because they fear losing funding and the relationship they have built with the sending churches.

Their fear is not baseless. Sophie Otiende, who works with a charity organization called Haart Kenya that rehabilitates trafficked children back with their families, explained that her refusal to allow volunteers to meet with vulnerable children meant less donations. She said, "There is a desperate need for funds, but if you want to work ethically then you pay a price."[30] Otiende's observation reveals the mixed motives that westerners

27. Lu, "Why There's A Global Outcry Over Volunteering At Orphanages."

28. Government of Kenya, *Guidelines for the Alternative Family Care*, 5.

29. ACC International, *Protecting Children: In Short-Term Missions*.

30. Grant, "Outcry Over 'Saviour Complex.'"

may have in supporting RCIs. Those giving funds want to help, but they also feel entitled to a certain kind of emotional experience, to the hugs and smiles and tears of "orphans." Some participants in STMS are motivated by the good feeling of caring for children in need, but they only want that role temporarily, without any long-term, truly life-altering commitment. Time and funds given from these mixed motives are not transformational, they are transactional: you give money, you get access to an emotional high.

Resistance to ending "orphanages" in Africa also comes from a paternalistic perspective—from the familiar narrative of the westerner "saving the helpless Africans." It's a perspective that makes the "helping" group feel better about themselves by feeling superior. It's a perspective that leads to the exploitation of children. And it's a perspective that degrades the Kenyan people by assuming they are not capable of enacting positive change within their own communities. One only has to consider the expertise of Stephen Ndung'u, Peter Kamau Muthui, Stephen Ucemebe, and Sophie Otiende above to see that Kenyans better understand their own problems and are better equipped to discern solutions that will work. Western churches need to let go of a paternalistic perspective in order to create coequal partnerships with Kenyans. More honest, coequal conversation with Kenya partners could focus on questions like:

- What organizations and programs should we fund? Which ones should we steer clear of funding?

- What is the best way to structure this program so that the children, families, and communities benefit?

- What difficulties are you encountering when trying to trace and reunite children with their families?

- How can we help you strengthen these children's families?

- What programs should we prioritize for funding?

- What can I help you with that the community is already doing?

- What problem are you having that I can help solve?

- How have the contributions I have made been helpful? Unhelpful?

Asking—and truly listening to the answers to such questions—creates the foundation of a global, copowering partnership. The traditional model of STMs—with youth and unskilled members of the church sent to play with the kids, shower them with gifts, post pictures on social media, and then leave after less than two weeks—does not help Kenyan children. But that doesn't mean that global partnerships should cease. As an alternative to the traditional STM, here are just a few of the ways that the western church can partner with Kenyans for the benefit of children:

1. Send trained professionals who have skills in counseling vulnerable children, helping trace families, or training family members on how to develop skills that generate income. It is best to send professionals who intend to build long-term relationships with the staff of these local organizations, training and teaching them best practices. It is far more effective to send just two or three people and redirect the rest of the funding towards the cause you are addressing.

2. Start an exchange program where two or three Kenyans receive funding to visit a western church, receive training from skilled kinship-care professionals, and see the effectiveness of the best practices they are learning.

3. Fund care provided by skilled Kenyan professionals who are ready to help the children in these homes. Otiende notes that "For the cost of a flight from the United States to Kenya, we could pay for a senior psychotherapist to treat around twenty children and families a month."[31]

Just as it took the West decades to phase out their own version of RCIs, so too will that process take time in Kenya. Fortunately, copowering collaborations like those listed above will enable Kenyans to benefit from the experience of the West in the transition to a kinship-care model. At the same time, western churches gain the opportunity to grow in humility as they become true partners in caring for the needs of vulnerable children.

Of course, this new ethos that we are recommending to churches and nonprofits goes far beyond matters of orphan care alone. Compassionate westerners who want to make a difference in any area of need in the world would do well to practice more mutuality and respect in intercultural partnerships, and more imaginative, context-informed approaches to addressing actual needs as defined by those who live in the context. Only then, in this work of re-visioning, might they learn to stand alongside their brothers and sisters in other nations, and to understand themselves as coequal members of the wider global church whose purpose it is to enact God's love and mercy for the whole world.

31. Grant, "Outcry Over 'Saviour Complex.'"

Gloria Kennedy

Gloria Kennedy is from Kenya and Tanzania. She has also studied and lived in America, Spain, and Thailand. She holds a BSc. in Business Administration, from Trinity University, San Antonio, Texas. She is also a GIA Graduate Gemologist. Gloria considers her faith, family, and friends as most important to her. When not spending time with loved ones she can be found reading, sampling new cuisines, watching documentaries, and hiking.

Buken Onyango

Buken Onyango is a community organizer, social entrepreneur, and a loving family man from Kenya. A decade of volunteer experience has given Buken the skillset needed to successfully work with youth on diverse community projects. Buken's experience and passion led him to co-found the Maisha Yangu Organization, based in Nairobi, Kenya. The community based organization supports children and youth by creating a safe space for them to access academic and artistic activities provided in the center. Buken believes that in order for communities to thrive, individuals must be willing to play their part towards effecting positive change.

Jeremy Cook

Jeremy serves as Pastor of Lavington Vineyard Church, a multicultural church of twenty-five nationalities in Nairobi, Kenya, where he has lived with his wife and three kids since 2014. He has a BA in Political Science from George Washington University, an MA in International Community Development from Northwest University, and a masters of divinity in Biblical Studies from Nairobi Evangelical Graduate School of Theology (AIU—Kenya). His studies have taken him to the intersection of social issues, global justice, theology, and the practical application of the good news of Jesus to everyday life. He loves sports, movies, and listening to podcasts while cooking or cleaning. As a social introvert, he loves hanging out with people, especially his family, but recharges best with a good book and a good cup of coffee, seated next to a crackling fire and his affectionate dog.

Andrea Sielaff

Andrea Sielaff works with The Seattle School of Theology and Psychology as a Researcher for Resilient Leaders Project and as adjunct faculty teaching Vocational Direction. In addition, she leads apprenticeship groups for MDiv students at Fuller Seminary. She was previously in campus ministry with InterVarsity Christian Fellowship, going on to earn a masters in Counseling degree from Northern Arizona University.

Bibliography

ACC International, *Protecting Children: In Short-Term Missions (A Guidance Manual and Toolkit for Churches and Christian Organizations)*, ACC International, 2016..

Anonymous Informant #1. Personal interview. 26 Jun 2020

Anonymous Informant #6. Personal interview. 02 Nov. 2020.

Bartelme, Tony. "Do No Harm? The Pros and Cons of Short-Term Missions." *The Post and Courier* (2020).

Batha, Emma. "Fact Box: Most Children in Orphanages are not Orphans." *Thomson Reuters* (2018).

Budd, Ken. "I Spent Time in a Kenyan Orphanage Hoping to Make a Difference. but was I Really Helping?" *WP Company* (2019).

CNN. "Orphanage 'Recruited Kids to Get Donations.'" *YouTube*, uploaded by EDOF, 14 Mar. 2017, www.youtube.com/watch?v=8xwQXXcvzjg.

Global Affairs Canada, *Taking Child Protection to the Next Level in Kenya*, UNICEF, Kenya, December 2015.

Government of Kenya, "Guidelines for the Alternative Family Care of Children in Kenya," *UNICEF* (2014).

Grant, Harriet. "Outcry over 'Savior Complex' fueling Exploitation of Kenyan Children." *The Guardian News and Media* (2018).

Kamau and Buken Onyango. Personal interview. 28 October 2020.

Lu, Joanne. "Why There's a Global Outcry over Volunteering at Orphanages." *NPR* (2020).

Mbakwe, Tola, "Christians Urged to Stop Volunteering in Orphanages as It Does More Harm than Good." *Premier Christian News* (2019).

Muthui, P. K. "Interview: My Childhood in a Children's Home." *Footsteps* 101, (2017).

Mwangi, Wagena. "Program to De-Institutionalize Children's Homes Roll Out." *Kenya News Agency*, (2018).

Sloth-Nielsen, Julia. "Kenya Takes Next Steps to Replace Children's Homes with Family Care." *The Conversation*, University of the Western Cape, (2019).

The Faith to Action Initiative, *Short-Term Missions: Guidance to Support Orphans and Vulnerable Children*. 2018.

United States Department of State. *Civilian Security, Democracy, And Human Rights: Child Institutionalization and Human Trafficking*. Office To Monitor and Combat Trafficking In Persons, Washington, 2018.

8

A Framework of Biblical Justice for Short-Term Missions

GENA RUOCCO THOMAS

MY SON CADEMON WAS born in Monterrey, Mexico, a highly industrialized city with Burger Kings, Starbucks, and several fine hospitals around. My husband and I had been living in Mexico teaching English and starting a coffee shop ministry. I had a Mexican doctor who studied in the States, spoke great English, and was one of the few doctors I could find who appreciated natural births. In 2006, the C-section rate of all births in Mexico was around 37.6% whereas typical national averages range between 10 and 15 percent.[1] Monterrey is one of the cities with the highest c-section rates worldwide. When my neighbors and fellow congregants saw me pregnant, they'd ask me when the date was. What they were not asking was: "When is the estimated due date of your baby?" like Americans ask. They were asking, "When is your scheduled c-section date for your baby?" I would often hear conversations of pregnant women saying things like, "I asked my doctor to schedule me on June fifth because that is my mother's birthdate."

---

1. Farland, "Use and Overuse."

During my pregnancy in Mexico, I read several pregnancy books. I could not get enough information into my academically-oriented brain. I researched things on the internet and asked lots of questions of the medical personnel I talked with. The pride of superiority quickly and easily crept up on me. I looked at other pregnant women as inferior and lacking significant knowledge on the medical ins and outs of childbirth. Sometimes I would have conversations with other women just to interject my knowledge of the process. Sometimes I would say nothing and walk away thinking, "She doesn't know anything." It wasn't until I read Bryant Myers' *Walking With the Poor* a year later that I realized how superior I had puffed myself up to be. According to Myers:

> When we fail to listen, to see what we can learn, we are in fact telling them that they are without useful information, without contribution. By dismissing what they know, we further mar the identity of the poor. Our good intentions deepen the poverty we seek to alleviate.[2]

In the majority of my conversations with women about pregnancy, I assumed they had nothing to offer. I believed that I couldn't learn anything from them. As far as I was concerned, everything I really needed to know, I had learned from my pregnancy books. I should be teaching them, I thought, and when the conversation wouldn't allow it, I felt like those conversations were a waste of my time.

My superior attitude gained no ground in the kingdom of God. How could it? Superiority means I have the power, and I don't need Christ's power. The word *superior* is a comparative of *superus* which means "situated above, upper."[3] I had put myself up on a pedestal of pregnancy books and looked down at my inferior, ignorant, pregnant peers. While I was troubled by the high rate of c-sections in Monterrey, I also came to realize that my attitude was not going to help that situation at all. I wonder how much I could have learned from my Mexican peers about pregnancy if I just listened to them. I was trying to be a walking billboard for natural-births—rather than a friend, a neighbor, a confidant.

2. Myers, *Walking with the Poor*, 144–45.
3. *Online Etymology Dictionary*, "Superior,"

Charity and the American Church

When we utilize a framework of charity for our short-term mission trips, we stand on the pedestals of our superiority, all the while allowing our arrogance to mar the good news of the gospel. The only thing we can boast in, says Paul, is "the cross of our Lord Jesus Christ, by which the world has been crucified to [us], and [we] to the world."[4] Myers contends that a superior attitude works like a "corrosive acid, eating away at our effectiveness in transformational development and Christian witness." [5]

That corrosive acid might be one of the enemy's favorite and most useful tools. Unfortunately, it's one we often embody during short-term missions, and it stems from a framework of American charity. In researching the word charity—outside of the King James Version where charity is translated from *agape love*—I found that the word *charity* as westerners typically use it today does not occur in the scriptures. In our contemporary Bible, there are thirteen biblical passages where the word "charity" is used. The most common verse (in several translations) that uses the English word charity is found in Acts 9:36, where Tabitha is described as "abounding in good deeds and acts of charity." The Hebrew translation of the original Greek word, according to the Orthodox Jewish Bible, is *tzedakah*, which is the word for justice which I will define in the next section. All thirteen cases actually translate to four more distinctive words than charity: *tzedek* (righteous, just), *tzedakah* (acts of justice), *nedavah* (donation), and *matanah* (gift).

Definitions of charity often involve the words *poor* and *in need*. Charity is an economically-loaded word. Power is assumed to be stronger in the one, the rich benefactor, than in the other—the needy beneficiary.[6] Benefactor and its synonyms all assume a power play:

- Benefactor—with the root *bene* (well) and *factor* (maker).

- Donor with the root *don* (gift).

- Patron with the root *lord/master/protector* maybe *father,* the foundation for words like *patronage, patronize*; even the foundation of the word *pattern*: a patron was a model to be imitated.

---

4. Gal 6:14 (AMPCE).

5. Myers, *Walking with the Poor,* 216.

6. The power differential built into the word is similar to the word "empowerment"—a dynamic of inequality that for which "copowerment"—a key term in this book—is the corrective.

Often short-term mission trips embody this framework of justice as groups of people are formed into the "haves" and the "have-nots," whether in tangible forms or by intangible means such as education, skills, theological and professional training, etc. While dealing with my own pregnancy in Mexico, I had made myself a "have" of intellectual superiority, while my Mexican neighbors were "have-nots" of that knowledge. However, that economic and intellectual bias is leveled out when mission-goers choose to view the world through a framework of biblical justice, a life of right relationships.

What Justice Is

Biblical justice is the act of practicing the "rightness" of God on earth, thereby making the future kingdom of heaven a present reality. Justice can be broken down into two main Hebrew words, *mishpat* and *tzedakah*. I appreciate Tim Keller's study of the concept of justice that can be found in his book *Generous Justice*. In the first chapter, he looks at these two Hebrew words. *Mishpat*, he explains, is "giving people what they are due, whether punishment or protection or care," and *tzedakah* is "a life of right relationships."[7] The two words are found together over thirty times in the Old Testament conveying the English concept of social justice.

Biblical justice includes several aspects: dignity, love, humanization, and shalom, but for the sake of this essay, I will focus on the concept of dignity.[8] Justice begins in Genesis 1, where dignity is automatically bestowed on every human being because of the innate *imago Dei* given when life is created. And it continues through the Bible. In Isaiah, we see that justice is a call on Christ's life: "Here is my servant, whom I uphold, my chosen one in whom I delight. I will put my Spirit on him, and he will bring justice to the nations."[9] And in the New Testament, we see Christ living out that call through the aspect of dignity in John 8, when the adulterous woman was brought before a group of people ready to stone her. In that moment, Christ did not preach from a platform of pride talking about how sinless *he* was, though he would have been justified in doing so. Christ, in fulfilling justice, brought dignity both to the woman's accusers by reminding them that they were not sinless, and to the woman by reminding her she was made in the image of God.

7. Keller, *Generous Justice*, 4–11.
8. For more, see my book, *Smoldering Wick*.
9. Isa 42:1 (NIV).

If part of the good news that Christ brought was the good news of dignity, then we also, as Christ-followers, must proclaim in word and deed a gospel that brings the good news of dignity. If our sermons are paternalistic, if our words come from a platform of pride, and if our deeds are done while undermining the people we *serve*, then we are not bringing true justice.

Additionally, a framework of justice allows the perceivable "haves" to understand mutuality as a calling, rather than a bonus, and requires them to step off their society-given pedestals. It allows the perceivable "have-nots" to understand they have much to bring to a short-term mission partnership and gives them the God-given right to step up to the same plateau as their western neighbors. When churches become communities that truly partner with one another as part of the global church, they take part in their divine role as the bride of Christ. When we begin to see justice as the Bible declares it to be, we are more equipped to take up Christ's call to faithfully bring forth justice through our short-term mission trips.

How Short-Term Trips Can Embody Justice

So, what does justice practically look like in short-term missions? Here, I offer two tools for participating in justice-minded short-term mission trips. The first tool, a typology of participation, scrutinizes the "what" of short-term trips through a better understanding of our concept of "participation." This is important because as we lean into justice, we must work to knock down pedestals. One major way to do so is to pay close attention to what type of participation we are asking from our partners who receive short-term teams. The second tool, a partnership analysis, scrutinizes the "how" of our short-term trips through a better understanding of our relationships with the host communities. If justice signifies a life of right relationships, we should be seeking right relationship with our partners.[10]

Typology of Participation

One of the first steps toward more participatory short-term mission trips is an awareness of types of participation. The following information comes from Jules Pretty, Professor of Environment and Society and Deputy

10. For more tools and ideas, see my book, *A Smoldering Wick: Igniting Short-Term Missions with Sustainable Practices.*

Vice-Chancellor at the University of Essex in England. Pretty includes seven types of participation. For the sake of this essay, you will see three. Each type of participation and its definition is taken directly from Pretty's *Typology of Participation: How People Participate in Development Programmes and Projects.*[11] The STM examples are case studies I have created to gain a better understanding of how these types of participations look in STM work, using an example of a North Carolina church connecting with a church in Monterrey, Mexico.

Manipulative Participation

Participation is simply a pretense, with "people's" representatives on official boards but who are unelected and have no power. Example: a North Carolina church tells a church in Monterrey, Mexico it plans to send a team to paint houses over the summer. The NC church asks the Monterrey church to come up with a list of ten people's houses they can paint. The NC church never asks if there are other needs within the church's community or if painting these houses will address any need at all. They simply ask for the list of ten houses and plan the trip accordingly. The pretense is that the Monterrey church is "participating" by choosing the ten.

Participation for Material Incentives

People participate by contributing resources (for example, labor) in return for food, cash or other material incentives. Farmers may provide the fields and labor, but are involved in neither experimentation nor the process of learning. It is very common to see this called "participation," yet people have no stake in prolonging technologies or practices when the incentives end. Example: the NC church asks the Monterrey church to have those who want their houses painted to contribute to the labor of their house being painted, whether by cooking for the team or by painting themselves.

Interactive Participation

People participate in joint analysis, development of action plans and formation or strengthening of local institutions. Participation is seen as a right,

11. Bass, Dalal-Clayton, and Pretty, *Participation in Strategies,* 32.

not just the means to achieve project goals. The process involves interdisciplinary methodologies that seek multiple perspectives and make use of systemic and structured learning processes. As groups take control over local decisions and determine how available resources are used, they have a stake in maintaining structures or practices. Example: the NC church has invested in relationships with members from the Mexican church prior to this STM trip. The two groups have decided that there is a sincere need for house painting among a group of church members. The two churches work together equally throughout the planning, implementing, and evaluating of this house-painting project. Together, with the Mexican church leading the discussion, they determine who should get their house painted and why, so that when neighbors ask why they can't have their house painted, the locals have a good reason, and jealousy is minimized.

Examining a group's current work in light of the different types of participation will help them discover whether or not they are involved in authentically participatory mission trips. Helpful questions include:

1. Which category does your church's current mission trips fall under?

2. Are projects fully planned before discussing them with the receiving communities?

3. If your group is currently involved in manipulative participation or participation through material incentives, what steps can be taken to move toward interactive participation?

Partnership Analysis

Humility is key to evaluating our current or future partnerships. Human beings are creatures of habit. It's easier to do things the way they have always been done, rather than to change. But, when we act out of humility, we can use reflection and evaluation to overcome our innate resistance and inspire positive change. A partnership analysis is simply a way of evaluating a partnership between two communities. As important as it is to evaluate an actual project, it is just as important to evaluate a relationship. Short-term missions should stem out of the Hebrew definition of *tzedakah*, as a life of right relationships. Partnership analysis is a tool toward accomplishing justice-based missions work from the start.

At the end of this article is the partnership analysis questionnaire in English.[12] Both churches, the sending and the receiving can fill this out, and then compare and discuss the answers between the leaders. If the churches are already in deep relationship with each other, this may feel very natural. If the conversation feels awkward, that's okay. No relationship gets deep without any awkwardness, and if we truly believe that justice is built on relationships, then these conversations are more important than the projects themselves. This form is meant to spark conversation more than it is meant to create additional paperwork for already-full filing cabinets.

After both churches fill out the form, a discussion afterward is critical.[13] What happens if the two churches answer this analysis differently? What happens if the sending church believes the partnership to be effective while the receiving church believes it to be paternalistic and negative? Or vice versa? If one church feels the partnership is negative, the two need to discuss possible changes. If sending or receiving churches are not willing to hear the other's side or not willing to change anything, it might be better for the partnership to end. While I would rather see the churches reconcile than separate, if these short-term missions are not rooted in *tzedakah* within the two churches, they cannot produce fruit that produces justice. "Either make the tree good and its fruit good, or make the tree bad and its fruit bad, for the tree is known by its fruit." [14]

Conclusion

The irony of my pregnancy with Cademon is that on a very hot day in August, he was born through C-section. My water broke around 2 a.m., and when contractions still hadn't started at 9 a.m. I went to see my doctor in Monterrey. Around 1 p.m., I was induced and by 11 p.m., Cade wasn't budging. His head was too big and my hips, amazingly, were too small. A C-section was performed and at 11:37 p.m. I met my nine-pound bundle of joy.

When the fun of meeting my little man died down, and the new grandparents had returned to the States, I was annoyed that God would let me have a C-section. Why would He do such a thing? Didn't he know I

12. A Spanish version of the partnership analysis is available on my website, genathomas.com

13. It is important to note that the twenty questions are specific for a church-missions setting.

14. Matt 12:33 (ESV).

was the voice of reason to so many Mexican women? I could have been an example of the goodness of natural births to them. Now I had to tell them all it was a c-section. Essentially, my question was the same as Job's: How could God allow such an injustice? The answer was a beautifully created, healthy, baby boy who stared at me and depended on me for everything. Just as God answered Job, he answered me: "Who are you? Have you created this universe? Have you put the stars in the sky and the fish in the sea? Have you created a human being? Look at the work of my hands and recognize who I am."[15]

Utilizing a framework of justice for our short-term mission trips will encourage us to no longer stand on the pedestals of our self-presumed superiority. At the end of our trips, when all is said and done, is God asking us "Who are you? Have you put the stars in the sky and the fish in the sea?" Or is he telling us "Well done, you have truly served through mutuality and magnified the dignity of your neighbors." My now eight-year-old son is a constant reminder that God is a God of Justice who knocks down pedestals, opposes the proud (and the proud's agenda), and gives grace to the humble.[16] May we learn to bring justice in our short-term missions through our humility and our willingness to participate equally with our host partners.

Partnership Analysis (English)[17]

1. Why is your church involved in this partnership?

2. What would make this a successful partnership for your church?

3. What would make this an unsuccessful partnership?

4. What goals does your church have for this partnership? Are those goals clearly defined and realistic? Are the objectives to obtain those goals clear between both churches?

5. Is it clear between the two partners what resources each is responsible for while projects are in place?

15. Job 38 (ESV).

16. Jas 4:6 (ESV).

17. Much of this partnership analysis was based on a partnership assessment tool created by the International Development Research Centre for global health partnerships. That tool can be found here: http://www.ccghr.ca/resources/partnerships-and-networking/partnership-assessment-tool/.

6. Has communication between the two churches been open and efficient? How could this improve if it needs to?

7. Has it been clear what role each plays in this partnership? How would you describe your church's role? How would you describe your partner church's role?

8. Has it been clear how long this partnership will last, depending on the goals set out by the partnership?

9. Has this partnership created dependency on either side? What steps have been taken to make sure this hasn't happened or doesn't happen?

10. Has this partnership perpetuated paternalism? What steps have been taken to make sure this hasn't happened or doesn't happen?

11. What are the strengths of this partnership?

12. What are the weaknesses of this partnership?

13. What is the biggest challenge about this partnership?

14. If there were three things you would ask your partner church to do that they aren't currently doing, what would they be?

15. Do you feel like the majority of your church's members who participate in this partnership have their voices heard among the leaders?

16. Do you, as a leader in your church, feel like your voice is heard in the decision-making process of this partnership?

17. Would you describe this partnership as a healthy relationship? Why or why not?

18. How does this partnership compare with other partnerships you currently have or have had in the past?

19. Overall, is this a mutually beneficial partnership?

20. How important is it to you or your church that this partnership continue?

Gena Ruocco Thomas

Gena Thomas is a writer, a faith-wrestler, a wife, and a mom. She and her husband, Andrew, have been married for eleven years and they have two children, a nine-year-old boy and a five-year-old girl. Gena works as a program coordinator for the National Immigration Program at World Relief. She has been featured on NPR's *Morning Edition* and in *Christianity Today* among other publications, and published her first book, *A Smoldering Wick: Igniting Missions Work with Sustainable Practices* in 2016. Published in 2019, Gena's second book, *Separated by the Border: A Birth Mother, a Foster Mother, and a Migrant Child's 3,000-Mile Journey* unpacks the story of reuniting her Honduran foster daughter with her family after separation at the US border. *Alisa and the Coronavirus* is Gena's first children's book, self-published in April 2020.

Bibliography

Bass, Stephen, Barry Dalal-Clayton, and Jules Pretty. "Participation in Strategies for Sustainable Development." *International Institute for Environment and Development* (1995).

Farland, L. "The Use and Overuse of Cesarean Sections in Mexico." *University of Chicago*, (2011).

Keller, Timothy. *Generous Justice: How God's Grace Makes Us Just.* New York: Riverhead Books, 2011.

Myers, Bryant L. *Walking with the Poor: Principles and Practices of Transformational Development.* Maryknoll, NY: Orbis, 2014.

Thomas, Gena. *A Smoldering Wick: Igniting Missions Work with Sustainable Practices.* United States: Gena Thomas, 2017.

Discussion Questions

THE FOLLOWING QUESTIONS ARE *meant to create "conversation" between this section's themes and your own perspectives and experiences. They are intended to be useful for both sides of the STM relationship: guests who travel to serve other communities, and the hosts who receive them. While these questions offer thought-provoking prompts for journaling, meditation, and prayer, they also serve as starting places for group discussion with others in your community who care about reimagining STM. We highly recommend both modes of engagement when that is possible.*

1. Is there a cultural lens that you once viewed the world through, but that you had to set aside for a different perspective? It is difficult to identify those elements of our worldview that don't serve us or others well. What are some ways that we can open ourselves to learning better ways to see?

2. Have you ever been in a situation where someone assumed that they were "the hero of the story" when in fact they should have been "standing in the back?" How did that make you feel? What do you think their motives were? In a short-term mission context, what can the host community do to help visitors better understand the roles they should play? Why might this be a difficult thing to do for leaders in the host context?

3. When you read in this section about the impact of colonial history, racism, or economic inequality on short-term missions, how did it make you feel? Is it difficult to acknowledge the ways in which social injustice has shaped current STM practices? Why?

4. If you are involved in hosting teams: were there particular issues raised in this section that caused you to see ways in which your actions and attitudes toward those teams are unhealthy or inauthentic? If you have been part of an STM team: did these chapters call to mind any ways that you or your teammates might have slipped into dishonoring or even oppressive behaviors without realizing it?

5. Do you agree that humility and repentance need to be part of the process of reimagining short-term missions? How might that make the global church better able to disrupt the STM status quo with creative alternatives?

6. If your church or community has an ongoing STM relationship, consider proposing that representatives of both the host and the sending context complete Gena Thomas's partnership analysis. What might make one side or the other hesitant to answer the analysis questions with frankness?

SECTION THREE

Curiosity and Teachability

As WILL BECOME CLEAR, the curiosity and teachability that this book's contributors exemplify informs the ideas they propose and the stories that they tell. They seek to learn new ways of understanding that will inspire new ways of being and doing. In some ways, "teachable" is almost too passive a word to describe this quality; "proactively curious" is a better term, because it suggests that those who are committed to rethinking STM are driven to seek hard after new knowledge in order to reimagine what is and dream of what could be. This sort of essential teachability requires courage, because what we receive when we open ourselves to the as-yet-unknown can make us feel insecure. And any of us with leadership responsibilities understand what courage it takes to introduce a new idea when it is likely to be perceived as a threat to tradition, stability, and even community identity. Yet teachable leaders help their people to be teachable as well—in truth, a crucial attitude to cultivate in every aspect of faith life.

We cannot hope to repair and reinvent our broken STM dynamic unless all stakeholders—especially those from sending contexts—choose to acknowledge what they do not yet know and embrace the stance of learners. In order to understand before we presume to act, we must learn to ask: What is required to truly, deeply listen to the people and places that make up the global church? How do foreigners learn to appreciate local wisdom, and honor the perspectives of their hosts? Those who receive short-term teams too must choose to be boldly curious, and to ask about the true needs and agendas of short-term mission participants.

Importantly, many of those who write for this essay collection speak from the receiving end of the church's well-meaning missional efforts. Too often the voices from these host cultures tend to be ignored by the sending church; if and when their perspectives *are* sought out, there are usually unspoken limitations on how honest they can be (or think they can be) due to the tricky dynamics of power and resource imbalances that are the source of so many problems in intercultural relations. Nevertheless, in this text we assert that those who receive short-term teams have critical contextual knowledge that we cannot do without if we want to serve effectively and to avoid doing damage. Therefore, in the next chapters, host perspectives are highlighted, as well as examples of sending churches who strive to remain curious and teachable in their global mission endeavors.

9

Resistance and Reconciliation

Towards a New Paradigm for STM

COREY GREAVES, *with* LENORE THREE
STARS *and* DOUG VOLLE

I'VE BEEN A YOUTH pastor for thirty years, with twenty-five spent on the Yakama Reservation. In that time, I've witnessed hundreds of short-term trips to the reservation. Each trip repeated the same tired pattern: groups began arriving at the beginning of June for week-long stints, continuing every week through August. By summer's end, hundreds of people had passed through the reservation in the fulfillment of their call to short-term "mission."

During each visit, groups would hold their vacation bible schools or kids's clubs, ostensibly to get a bunch of little Natives "saved." They might also paint houses and clean up yards in the community—though rarely would they take the time to create relationships with the people who lived in these places. It was enough for them to collect photos of themselves doing the Lord's work, or selfies with the Native kids they were evangelizing—critically important images for the slide presentations for the folks back home. Week after week for the whole summer, more groups would arrive to paint more houses, clean more yards, get the same kids "saved" all over again and then go home feeling good about their accomplishments.

As well-intentioned as these short-term visitors might have been, their presence never really changed much on the reservation. And while they might have left feeling good about themselves, their visits were not so good for the Native people who hosted them. This had everything to do with the way they looked at the Yakama people: by defining our community as a "mission field," they unintentionally communicated the message that we were essentially needy; relegated to being only receivers rather than givers in a mutual relationship.

I once watched as two little girls showed up at one of the STM kids's club events at a reservation park. From their appearance, it was obvious they had been having a wonderful time playing in the dirt, as kids anywhere might do. One of the white teenagers running the event began brushing the dust off the little Yakama girls, crooning "Oh, you poor things! I wish I could just take you home with me!" As I watched this culture clash play out, the message was loud and clear: the short-term visitors thought that what they had to offer our kids was better than what we could ever give them. It was the message implied by every group, all the time: we were the humble receivers, and they were the blessed givers. Through these kinds of encounters, the shorter-term visitor communicates to the Native people, "We don't need you. You can add nothing of value to our lives. But we, on the other hand, have everything of value to bestow upon you."

Disrupting Bad Practices

Partly as an act of resistance to this flawed perspective, we started Mending Wings—a nonprofit Native youth organization located on the Yakama Reservation in Washington State. We work to empower Native American youth and families to walk together in wholeness and beauty, to honor Creator through our cultures and lives, and to promote healing and wholeness through our programs. We also aim to share with others the life-changing hope we find as followers of the Jesus way.

One of the ways that Mending Wings shares that hope with those outside of our community is by offering an alternative to the "short-term mission" experience through a program we call SLAM (Students Learning About Missions). SLAM trips were born out of resistance to STMs—a mainstream practice that more often than not perpetuates false impressions among non-Natives and demeans indigenous people. As we've sought to disrupt conventional STM praxis, we have learned that a better approach to engaging teams from mainstream churches is essentially invitational; that we as the receiving community must set the agenda for short-term trips; and that we can offer the gifts of new perspective to help our visitors world views to be more complete. While we don't claim that SLAM trips should be a universal model that can be employed in every host context, we do believe that there are elements that can be recontextualized by other Native American and First Nations people . . . and perhaps even by other indigenous groups elsewhere in the world.

Invitation Versus Imposition

SLAM trips were born out of the desire to see short-term mission trips to Native reservations radically altered. Mending Wings organizes and coordinates these trips and, most importantly, *invites* interested youth groups to the reservation. While this might seem like a relatively small shift in STM thinking, it does in fact represent a fundamental challenge to the typical model, whereby visiting groups assume their presence is wanted and needed. Instead, a SLAM trip is dependent on an invitation extended by representatives of the Yakama community. Rather than "targeting" an "underserved" or "needy" context, groups that are interested in the Yakama context might at best inquire about a visit, but then must subsequently wait to be invited into a relationship of *copowerment* by their hosts. It is a relationship of coequality and mutual respect, grounded in the assumption that each stakeholder group has something to learn from the other.

This reorientation to an invitational approach has made it easier for us to resist the pressure of politeness, and to actually say no to some prospective teams. In the process of preparing teams for their visit, SLAM staff are careful to explain that participants should never impose their presence on another community, and that visits must be guided and mediated by people who represent that community. That means in some cases that a visiting team should be prepared for the option of being turned away. If for example we sense that a prospective team is committed to the conventional STM goal of "Christianizing" indigenous people, we will not invite them to spend time with us. Indigenous peoples in North America have experienced profound abuse, genocide, and cultural destruction at the hands of missionaries who have sought to dominate us in their zeal for conversion. If a Native person gets any sense that a sending church might be framing the short-term trip in the objectifying terms of conversion (as opposed to simply bearing witness to Creator's work in their lives), any sort of relationship becomes impossible, and that group will never be invited to come learn with us.

Teaching Trust

When it comes to hosting teams of visitors, one of Mending Wings's objectives is to shift the balance of power—from a one-directional, top-down dynamic to a mode that is more mutual and respectful. In our approach, the short-term visitor is no longer a "missionary" in the conventional sense of the word; instead, we help that person to become a learner who at the very least recognizes a void in their cultural understanding of Native people. Thus, we shape the expectations of every short-term trip to emphasize *learning about the Yakama context* as the primary objective. Importantly then, we are the ones who define the learning objectives and agenda of each trip, since we are the ones who know our context and culture best. While we do involve our visitors in service projects, we also build into those experiences some opportunity to build relationships with people in our community. This reorientation of the typical power dynamic of short-terms missions allows us to build healthier, more mutually respectful relationships between the visiting teams and their Yakama hosts.

In a typical visit, leaders in our community plan cultural immersion activities, including an Indigenous worship circle, a frybread and salmon meal with traditional drummers and dancers, and opportunities to try Native crafting techniques. An important part of the learning experience is the reservation tour, during which they learn the stories and the historical meanings attached to our key landmarks; during this time, we also curate interactive discussion about the painful legacy of missionary influence among our people, and about efforts toward conciliation between the American Church and Native America. In these ways, we make learning from Indigenous teachers and community leaders the main component of this new missional model we have been designing.

Several days of the SLAM week involve community service projects that are chosen in advance by elders in our community. This sometimes meets with resistance in the visiting team leaders, who have become used to determining their group's agenda. However, when non-Natives choose to recognize the authoritative role that elders have in Yakama society, they not only honor those elders—they also raise the status of the elders in the eyes of the community as a whole and demonstrate respect for the culture. In so doing, those who represent authority from mainstream contexts convey the message to the Yakama people that "mission" must be done *with* the people, rather than *to* them.

By having our elders determine the service projects for STM groups, we ensure that the work will be relevant and useful to our community. At the same time we help groups to avoid the common mistake of impos- ing projects that prioritize their own preferences and priorities, or projects that allow them to stay within their own comfort zones. This approach is humbling by design, and challenges even the most servant-hearted teams to trust themselves to us—and to believe that we have their best interests at heart even as we protect the interests of the community.

Time has proven that our approach works well. Many of the older people in the community have expressed gratitude for the visiting teams's efforts in their houses and yards—not just for the work that was done, but also for the manner in which it was done. They appreciate the time we build into the schedule for the short-term visitors to sit and talk with the owners of the houses before they do any work for them. Here, there is similarity to Robert Katende's insight into the Ugandan culture interacting with Ameri- can visitors, and having to teach visiting teams to reorient what they believe about time and relationships.[1] In our context, even this seemingly small act of prioritizing relationship requires intentionality, and we find we must begin early in a team's orientation process to help them to learn (and hope- fully embrace) our value of relationship-building over "getting stuff done."

The Gift of New Perspective

If STM visitors can get past thinking of our people as "the mission field," SLAM trips provide the opportunity for them to consider the possibility that the Yakama people too are and have always been beloved by Creator . . . and to understand that Creator has *always* been at work among our people from the beginning. As a good friend and mentor once said, Creator did not come to this continent on the Mayflower. In truth, many Yakama cultural norms and traditions are actually congruent with the teachings of Yeshua. The core virtues of the Yakama Nation include honesty, compassion, re- spect, self-denial, service and purity. Our traditional feasts and ceremonies commend thankfulness to Creator, and celebrate devotion of the individual

1. See Robert Katende's observations in chapter 1 of this volume, 5–16.

to the communal good. These are truths we offer to those of our short-term visitors who have ears to hear.

One of the most important things that a SLAM trip participant experiences is exposure to Indigenous theological perspectives as alternatives to mainstream theologies that have been shaped by hellenistic influences and a western European worldview. We have found that when our brothers and sisters representing the dominant culture learn to question—and even deconstruct—entrenched western theological presumptions, new doors are opened to authentically conciliatory conversation.

For example, we will sometimes work with our short-term visitors to become aware of the kind of American cultural gnosticism that draws a hard line between material and spiritual realities, and encourages a devaluation of the material in relation to the spiritual. We contrast this dualism with the more integrated Yakama worldview, in which *all* creation, material and spiritual, is considered sacred, interconnected, and interdependent. There is spirit in all elements of Creation, human and nonhuman. From an indigenous perspective, we *are* that creation. We are not separate from it, as if Creation is *there* and we are over *here*. We have a saying, *"thlakwi inmi naynuma"*—all my relatives—a foundational truth that conveys this deep sense that we are connected to the world around us. The rightful role of human beings then is not to rule over or commodify creation. Rather, we must seek to coexist with and care for all our relations in the great family that is Creation—in a dynamic of *kin-dom* rather than kingdom.

Another significant dualism we help them to understand is the over-valuation of the divine over the secular that characterizes western Christian thought and practice. Throughout history, the mainstream church has dismissed what Native cultures consider sacred—like a song, an eagle feather, or a ceremony—and judged them as syncretism and idol-worship. Thus, Native people are deemed "savage" and "pagan," and by definition then become the object of the missional efforts to "save" them. This way of thinking has historically had disastrous consequences for Native peoples in North America. Yet even today, the relatively small number of Indigenous converts are conditioned to reject aspects of their own cultures as essentially sinful. This of course has everything to do with the fact very few Native people identify as Christian, despite (or because of) hundreds of years of missionary efforts.

When it is Better to Receive than to Give

Students who choose to accept our invitation to travel to the Yakama Nation and learn from us and other members of our community usually leave with a greater understanding of Creator. At the same time, they learn accurate historical perspectives that engender appreciation for the beautiful cultures of Native peoples. We hope too that their time with us helps them to have confidence to share their new understanding with others.

One student participant described his time on the reservation as "deeply personal and yet far bigger than myself, my youth group and my community as a whole." In another conversation, the pastor of that youth's church commented: "When our students come back from a SLAM trip, they are not the same. For many, their relatively narrow worldview gets deconstructed, and they see themselves with a little more humility; still others come to understand the pain of social inequality and systemic injustice in a whole new way. In the end we just stopped calling these trips "mission" trips because what they really ended up being were 'transformation trips.'"[2]

In fact, Mending Wings doesn't refer to these trips as "mission trips" at all, and we try to get the visiting teams to put aside that term because of the expectations and associations it implies. We make it very clear to prospective teams: "We invite you to come and learn. Your primary aim is not to bring something to us." That is not comfortable for most, and sometimes they'll counter with the question, "How can we help each other?" Yet even that well-intentioned question makes the assumption that both sides have just as much to give to the other—and frankly, that is not always the case. Sure, ideally churches from different cultural contexts should learn to collaborate and find ways to bless one another out of their respective strengths. Yet when the balance of power between cultures has been so unequal for so long, the way to correct it is to put a lot of weight on the other side of the scale.

In North America at least, the question churches should be asking indigenous people is simply, "Will *you* help *us*?" In order to be able to do that though, they must first recognize the incompleteness of their perspective that comes from not listening to the host people of the land they now inhabit. If they aren't humble enough to realize and acknowledge that their perspective is incomplete, then the question makes no sense to them. And until it does make sense, Native churches will continue to be the perpetual

---

2. All SLAM trip participant quotes were shared on the condition of anonymity.

mission field, the needy recipients, the unreached, the marginal—all that church missions language we throw around so flippantly. This "mission mentality" reflects historically-rooted assumptions about culture, power, and worth. What the mission mentality does *not* reflect is the understanding that all churches are equally worthy in their cultural distinctiveness, and that no church, regardless of its culture, is complete in itself.

To be clear, it's not just the STM visitors who gain on SLAM trips. The Yakama people experience benefits from SLAM trips, too—from the completion of service projects to being treated with respect by the trip participants. For many in the community, there is affirmation and healing when they experience cultural outsiders who do not come teaching "the right way," and who do not unthinkingly demean the Yakama culture in their efforts to help. It's a win-win paradigm shift, and one we hope to see replicated and contextualized in other Indigenous communities. And while we freely acknowledge the ways in which our guests serve the community, we make it clear to them that they must cultivate the humility to be served, and an open-heartedness that allows them to be changed by their encounter with the Yakama people. Because dominant STM culture too often emphasizes a one-way service dynamic that privileges STM participants, we contend that it is necessary to flip the script, and to call attention to what our visitors receive from the communities they serve. The ethos of SLAM trips then is a corrective to the cultural hubris that has caused most short-term trips to do more harm than good.

On some level, every SLAM trip we host on the reservation is an act of resistance against those aspects of short-term missions that work against the practical coequality of *all* peoples who love and follow Yeshua. When we share with our guests the trauma and loss that misguided missionary efforts have caused the Yakama people, both those with the courage to speak the stories and those with the courage to listen become collaborators in making space for a completely reimagined paradigm to displace conventional STMs. And as we create opportunities to engage one another in authentic curiosity and respect, we bring about cultural reconciliation that only mutual understanding makes possible. As one youth director of a visiting group testified, "We have built a relationship to keep learning and serving, bridging two cultures together and glorifying God in the process." If the lives of Native and non-Native people are seen as two separate rivers, it is our ultimate hope that in Yeshua the rivers can learn to flow together as one.

To all diverse peoples in the world—those who share a common
love for the One who made us all:
Tamánwiła, naknúwit chī mami wakíshwit.

Creator, bless these lives.

Corey Greaves

Corey Greaves is Blackfeet, Klickitat, and Irish and lives on the Yakama
Reservation in Washington State. He's the president and cofounder of
Mending Wings, a Native American, nonprofit youth organization. Corey desires to see Native youth and families restored to wholeness by the
strength of Yeshua, and he seeks to bring reconciliation between the Body
of Christ and Native people by addressing real issues, both historical and
contemporary. He and his wife, Gina, have four children: Steven, Kathleen,
Carissa, and Matea.

Lenore Three Stars

Lenore was born on Pine Ridge Reservation in South Dakota, where her
father was born. Her mother is Minnecoujou Lakota from the Cheyenne
River Reservation, South Dakota. Lenore received her BA from Fort Lewis
College in Durango, Colorado. Upon retiring from a federal civil rights
career in Seattle, she moved to Spokane to be an active *unci* (grandmother) to her two *takojas* (grandkids), and later earned an MA through the
North American Institute of Indigenous Theological Studies from Portland
Seminary/George Fox University in Oregon. Lenore speaks, writes and co-
facilitates for the annual Journey to Mosaic, a faith-based racial reconciliation experience in the Pacific Northwest. Lenore also serves on nonprofit
boards related to her interests in the local community (CupofCoolWater.
org), Justice (Evangelicals4Justice.org), Indigenous issues (Eloheh.org),
and a discipleship of creation care (Circlewood.online).

Doug Volle

Doug Volle is a graduate of the International Community Development
master's program at Northwest University. He participated in traditional
STMs and desires to leverage that experience to help Christ-followers

reframe how they view missions. He earned a bachelor of arts degree from Purdue University and served eight years in the United States Navy. He currently resides in Seattle, Washington.

10

Rethinking Short-Term Missions
In Partnership for a Better Way

Nathan Nelson

I WILL NEVER FORGET the experience of instructing a short-term mission team to move a pile of rocks from one side of a construction site to another. There was no real need for this task, aside from keeping a group of eager high schoolers and young adults busy and maintaining their expectations of working hard to serve the needy. As I considered the look of naïve satisfaction on their sun-burnt faces as they labored, I thought to myself, "Isn't there more to short-term missions than this?"

That was more than ten years ago—and I've been exploring that question ever since. After countless short-term trips to countries throughout Latin America, Eastern Africa, and the Caribbean—and after working from the host and organizational side as well as that of the sending church, I continue to wonder if any of the people we visit are actually better off as a result of our short-term efforts. Which is something that you might find ironic, given that I'm the missions pastor at my church. Yet I still have my doubts—as I am sure many of you do, given that you've chosen to pick up this book.

Like me, you might be stuck in an in-between place, knowing that STMs are messed up, but also having experienced enough that was *good* about short-term mission trips that you can't dismiss them out of hand. Indeed, for me it was a short-term mission trip that first ignited my passion for working among the vulnerable!

Still, I have to ask:

- *What do we really gain by continuing to send groups of foreigners around the globe to spend very limited time in communities unlike their own?*

- *What steps can be taken to mitigate the harmful outcomes that make us question the effectiveness of STMs to begin with?*

- *And what kinds of positive, genuinely transformational outcomes are within the scope of STMs?*

Frankly, whether you are a pastor, congregant, missions organization leader, leader in a host context, or member of a host community, I think we all need to be asking questions like these if we're ever going to develop creative solutions and find a better way forward. *Crucially, all these stakeholders need to be talking about such things together.*

That's what we've been trying to do in my community, Bethany Community Church (BCC) in Seattle. And as hard as it has been to confront some of the shadow sides of missions, the process has nonetheless given us hope that there are better ways possible. As a community, we at BCC try to maintain a posture of learning, so I can only tell you about the unfolding process we are in. In that process we have developed some particular practices that have radically changed the ways we engage in STM: as a community we have come to believe that key practices for STM done well include *long-term partnership, trusting collaboration (copowerment), and mutuality of impact ("reverse" mission).* Most importantly, in learning these things we've had our hearts changed, we think, to be in better alignment with Christ's mission in the world.

Long-Term Partnership

At Bethany Community Church we've come to believe that short-term mission efforts need to be rooted in the core conviction *that the sending church and the receiving community are called to do something together that cannot otherwise be accomplished apart.* Thus, at the heart and soul of STMs is the foundational practice of *partnership.* As we have sought to learn how to be good partners, we've learned that we must commit to the time it takes to build authentic, lasting relationships.

My current role overseeing global and local mission at BCC is in great part about cultivating these partnerships that are the key to our participation in Christ's mission in the world. Prior to this more relational stance, our church (like many others) had a small lay missions committee that stewarded the missions budget, parsing out funds to an extremely long list of individuals and organizations. While the heart behind the work was great, there was a lack of strategic objectives, accountability, and mutuality of impact. The situation prompted my predecessor to guide the church through an intensive process of self-evaluation that focused our giving on four key areas: (1) global mission partnerships, (2) local mission partnerships, (3) supported missionaries, and (4) local outreach ministries (i.e. community meals, food banks, etc.). Given the kind of investments that these more robust, mutual mission partnerships require, we chose to go deep with a select few organizations that seemed most aligned with our vision and values.

Since that time of reorientation, we've learned to look for resonance with the transformation goals of specific partner communities. Advisory teams composed of staff and lay people work with these mission partners to define the terms of our partnerships, and to coordinate our respective roles in working toward collaborative goals. All parties in our partnerships commit to an initial period of three years of working together; though in practice the average duration of these copowering relationships ranges from seven to ten years—the time it takes, we've discovered, to build the sort of authentic, community to community relationships that yield mutual transformation on both sides.

In an effort to describe just how effective and transformational this long-term relationship approach has been, I'll describe our longest standing global partnership—between BCC, and World Relief (WR) in the Musanze district of Rwanda. The mutually established objective of BCC and WR Rwanda is to create networks of local churches that act together as agents of holistic transformation in their communities. In the ten years we have been in partnership, this work has grown from an initial network of twenty local churches to more than one hundred and fifty churches from many denominations. This collaborative project now directly supports the social, emotional, spiritual, and physical well-being of more than one hundred and fifty thousand people in the Musanze region. From our coordinated efforts we have learned that when all parties are committed for the *long term*, the scope and quality of our plans improve. As a result, the impact and influence of WR Rwanda has steadily increased, and BCC has gained the opportunity (through STMs and consistent investment of resources) to be part of deep, enduring systemic change that has become apparent only over the course of several years of collaborative participation.

However, I want to be clear that our approach to partnership is more than transactional. That is, we believe that the church should aspire to be more than a "foundation" of sorts, distributing grants to "do-good" organizations around the world. When we think in terms of the *global* church, all faith communities (whatever their size) are uniquely positioned by God to co-labor with other faith communities—variously located and differently resourced—to accomplish together what each could not otherwise achieve apart from long-term, collaborative partnership. And that sort of impact for good in the world has everything to do with relationship.

Yet what does this imply for the practice of sending short-term teams? For us it means that STMs—*in the context of long-term partnerships*—are never one-off experiences; rather, as we have experienced, trips to our partners can become highly anticipated visits between friends. When we send teams to Rwanda, we always have participants who have gone on prior trips. Those who are first-time team members are welcomed into an ongoing relational story, and a legacy of effective partnership involving many co-laborers who have been working in concert toward common goals over many years. For BCC this approach has represented a dramatic paradigm shift away from what Bryant Myers calls the "God-complex"—the belief that holistic transformation is within the scope of a single person, a single trip, or a single project. We have instead become believers in the power of copowering, long-term partnerships as a better means of living out Christ's missional call.

Copowerment and Trust

In keeping with this sort of global church mindset, the BCC/WR partnership grew out of a high valuation on mutuality. To more accurately reflect this stance in our practice, we made an intentional choice to change the term "mission trips" to "strategic visits." This language was chosen for two primary reasons. First, all of our trips are now oriented around the advancement of *shared, mutually-crafted strategic objectives*. Second, the term "visit" was chosen for its implicit boundaries around the role of STM visitors in the context of the ongoing work on the ground: a STM trip is not *the* work, nor is it expected to alter (or interfere with) the trajectory of the work already in progress. Instead, we define our objectives for *strategic visits* to our global partners as follows:

- *Support and encourage* the mission organization's staff in the work they are doing.

- *Share the team members's unique gifts* as they align with the ongoing work in the host context.

- *Broaden the understanding* of the BCC team members with regard to: (1) issues of poverty, justice, and the role of the Gospel, and (2) the specific issues people face in the geographic area of focus.

- *Equip visiting team members to be ambassadors* for the partnership, and to communicate to the larger BCC community about what they have experienced upon their return.

Within this framework for strategic visits, we have seen much mutual learning and growth over the course of ten years of partnership with WR Rwanda. At one point, for example, one of our team members with experience in orphan and vulnerable children care (OVC) identified and proposed an opportunity to grow WR's programming to meet this area of significant need in Rwanda. In the two years that followed, BCC provided support for WR staff members to receive and integrate training in best OVC practices from outside organizations. Monthly consultation calls took place between BCC's staff and lay leadership who had expertise in this area, culminating in WR's adoption and integration of a new training program that they began to implement in-country. This training was not only widely adopted throughout the rest of Rwanda, but also adapted for implementation by WR in other contexts around the world.

In addition—and in accordance with BCC's emphasis on investing in the growth of staff and leadership in its partner communities—WR invited BCC teams to participate in its annual all-staff retreat in Rwanda. Pastors and lay people from BCC worked alongside WR's national leadership to plan and conduct a four-day overnight retreat as a core component of its visit. The first year we participated in the retreat, out of six formal sessions, our team formerly participated in just two of them. The majority of our engagement happened instead through mingling with Rwandese staff during meals and downtime, praying with one another during breakout sessions, learning from the presenters when it was appropriate to participate in meetings, and of course (as one does in Rwanda), dancing together. In the following year, visiting BCC partners were invited to take on a little more responsibility, leading a formal teaching time as well as a time of testimonials. In the third year, we had earned enough trust (and had learned enough about the context and the needs) to be able to cocreate multiple sessions with the WR Rwanda retreat planning committee, co-leading sessions with them around the topics of staff development to meet needs that they had identified. Each time our level of involvement was changed, we were able to bring BCC team members with the specific skills to meet the expressed needs of our partners.

Recently I got an email from WR's church partnership liaison, who wrote, "Nathan, we are hoping that your team from BCC will *not* participate in next year's retreat." For a moment my heart sank through my office chair. What had we done to hurt the relationship (despite our best intentions)? As I read on though, my fears were relieved: our Rwandan partners were in fact simply reframing our role. It turned out WR was asking us, instead of directly participating ourselves, to equip another international church partner of theirs to engage in the retreat as part of its annual visit, broadening the participation of its various partners in this effective, collaborative, mutually-impactful way of working with one another in the context of STMs.

What I hope you can see here is that even after many years of partnership, we still needed to continue to build trust and maintain a learning posture as we copowered one another. In that process, they changed us even as we influenced them. With time, and with each visit, the relationships deepened, and opportunities for shared transformation increased. Over the years, our work together has strengthened and expanded the work in Rwanda, and helped to develop the spiritual maturity of the WR staff. At the same time, the BCC community has learned the power of humility and teachability, and we continue to experience the privilege of using our gifts and resources in significant, life-changing endeavors that help us to live out our missional calling.

"Reverse" Missions

When we embrace God's call to mission, we become part of a shared story of God's movement in the whole world; we are all members of the global church. I am convinced after over ten years of involvement in STM's around the globe that Christ's mission is neither entirely "global" nor "local" in nature. While at BCC we are invested in what many term "foreign" missions, we also understand that God calls us as a community to be light in our local contexts through active engagement with local government, businesses, schools, community initiatives, and nonprofits. In an effort to stop seeing global and local mission as entirely unique modes, we have been developing partnerships that blur the boundaries and integrate our various missional engagements.

This has meant actively welcoming the input and influence of our global church partners. By cultivating an awareness of our own needs and limitations, and practicing a stance of teachability, we make it possible for our global partners to be strong for us in the places we are not. This of course flies in the face of the assumption of superiority that is at the heart of American culture in particular; we are taught to assume that our ways are always better, and that mission is essentially a one-way transfer of resources to the objects of our mission projects.

As an example of this opening of ourselves to the shaping influences of our global mission partners, I'll share about the inspiration we've received from the work of WR in Rwanda. Specifically, our partners helped us to see our need to be in partnership with other regional churches here at home in the Seattle area, and from the Rwandan model we were able to draw practical methods to help us gather a coalition of disparate churches united around a common purpose. The more that representatives of BCC witnessed that sort of purposeful unity in Rwanda, the more we realized as a church that we needed a similar dynamic in our home context.

BCC is sandwiched between one of the wealthiest neighborhoods in Seattle, and a commercial corridor characterized by drug use, homelessness, and prostitution. Our church has a number of outreach ministries designed to serve folks experiencing these areas of brokenness. The same is true of several other churches nearby. The challenge has been that all these churches and ministries have tended to be invested in their own projects and causes; despite occasional attempts at working together over the years, we've had little success at coordinating our efforts and sharing resources across congregational lines.

This turned out to be a perfect opportunity to entrust ourselves to the strengths of our international partners. As part of BCC's partnership with WR in Rwanda, each year we are visited in Seattle by the WR Country Director, Moses Ndahiro. On one of his visits Moses asked me if I would introduce him to people working in local ministries among the poor and marginalized—so I set up a meeting involving folks from our church, as well as representatives of a local ministry that worked primarily with people experiencing homelessness in the neighborhood. At this gathering, Moses asked thoughtful, challenging questions—made all the more provocative by his unique East African perspective and his experiential wisdom. He led us in a powerful conversation that revealed our common compassion for the vulnerable and revealed new thinking about how area churches might rally around our common cause of serving the unhoused poor.

That meeting was the beginning of a new approach to serving the vulnerable—based on the core themes of unity and collaboration that had been modeled for us by our WR partners in Rwanda, but contextualized to a neighborhood in Seattle through what could be thought of as a "reverse missions" trip. The lessons taught to us by our Rwandan partners inspired and equipped us for powerful, honest, reconciling conversations with area churches and ministries. The new and stronger partnerships that resulted allowed the mutual sharing of our respective resources and capacities, and have made all of us more effective at meeting the needs of the local poor.

It is important to note, as my dear friend Moses pointed out, that the very language of "reverse" trip is imperfect in that it implies something about the practice that is counter to the norm—so we use the term provisionally, and temporarily. You see, while the practice of reverse mission might be new at BCC, it is our hope that trips going both ways will someday become the norm—and become yet another means by which we can experience greater mutual transformation that comes as a result of genuine, reciprocal relationships.

Reversing the Short-Term Mission Model

Sylvia Ramquist

In the early 2000s, the staff at Westminster Chapel in Bellevue, Washington began to ponder new ways for our church community to reach out to those living in our neighborhoods. An idea was formed for our nearly all-white church to throw a Lunar New Year (LNY) party for the Asian residents in Bellevue. Many of these neighbors couldn't return home to celebrate the one holiday that wraps together the significance of our western celebration of Thanksgiving, Christmas and Easter in one huge homecoming event. As we prayerfully considered how to invest in our multicultural community, we decided that instead of traveling to another country on a short-term trip, we would invest in the represented cultures in our city. Likewise, rather than landing in a new community with our own agenda, we focused on the interests of our neighbors and set out to serve them by celebrating in their own context. And thus, Lunar New Year became our first Reverse Short-Term Mission Trip.

At first, we had no clue how to celebrate the LNY, but we learned. Our first celebration included family fun, decorations, folk songs, a program with dances, and plenty of food. Knowing only a handful of people to invite, we planned for one hundred and fifty people—and around three hundred showed up! We quickly ran out of food! While we were mortified, we realized we'd found a need in our local community. There were happy tears, and notes of gratitude that an American congregation would care about the Asian community enough to serve them in this manner. It was important for our congregation to work outside of the traditional outreach models and build relationships with our neighbors by meeting these felt needs.

We continued our LNY celebrations, and over the next twelve years the event grew in size and scope, but always with a trust-building goal. We invited the top local folk-dance troupes to perform, invited helpful organizations to host booths with multi-language materials (the County Library, YMCA, City Hall, etc.) as well as local ethnic church groups. Most recently, the Bellevue mayor opened the program, Microsoft sponsored a ping-pong tournament, and our senior pastor gave a short talk that set the calendar animal of the year in a biblical context. It was a by-the-community, for-the-community event that annually drew around eighteen hundred participants.

As a result of our small idea, we have enjoyed an increase of trusted relationships in the spheres of business, non-profit, and government. We began to see a large influx of Asian Christians and non-Christians coming to other programs we offered, like Alpha, VBS, and weekly worship services. Our neighbors also started to get involved in serving because they felt seen and valued at Westminster through our Lunar New Year connections.

While many in our congregation were dubious or even dissenting at the beginning, believing we were inviting demonic forces through zodiac and money-influenced events into our sacred space, we prayerfully continued to invite our congregation to participate in this Reverse Short-Term Mission opportunity. The impact was tangible in breaking down preconceptions and prejudices. We were thrilled to begin to transform from an "us-to-them" to a "we" missional worldview through volunteering together, learning from each other, and laughing over mutual mistakes and misunderstandings.

Sylvia Ramquist

Sylvia Ramquist grew up in a missionary family, invested twenty years as a missionary in Japan, and served in local and global mission leadership at Westminster Chapel in Bellevue, Washington. She now resides in California with her husband, grown children, and grandchildren.

We Won't Give Up

I believe that among others, these three main elements of our global missions program offer some hope for establishing new paradigms for future STM praxis. The uneasiness with conventional short-term missions that I confessed from the start is still very real for me. Yet that dissatisfaction has pushed me and my fellow discontents at Bethany Community Church to try something new. So, if there is anything you take from this account, my hope is that you will be motivated to trust your own misgivings about the ways we've been doing STM, to shake up the status quo of your own community, and to find the courage (and creativity) to try something new. Ideally, you'll do this revolutionary work in partnership, alongside Christ-followers whom you might have previously consigned to "the mission field" (which poses the question, were these ever coequal partners at all?). As messy and unproductive as STMs can be, I for one am not willing to give up on the practice quite yet. Until I've seen a better way for my church to pursue the missional call, I am not ready to give up on my belief that STM's are indeed a means by which God's people can participate in making real the kingdom of Christ in this world. And so, I press on—with my church family, with local ministry partners, and with our partners in different parts of the world—trying new things and attempting to discern the next thing God might have in mind for us as we seek to love and serve together.

Nathan Nelson

Nathan Nelson is the Pastor of Mission and Outreach at Bethany Community Church in Seattle, Washington. He has years of experience working in short-term missions on the side of the sending church and of the receiving organization. He holds a master's of Divinity with an emphasis in International Development and Urban Studies from Fuller Theological Seminary, and bachelor of arts in Global Development and Sociology from Seattle Pacific University. He calls the Pacific Northwest home and lives every day in gratitude and admiration for his beloved wife Maci.

11

The Vandalism of Education
in Short-Term Trips

Scott Bessenecker *with* Fr. Benigno Beltran

Mark Twain said, "Travel is fatal to prejudice, bigotry, and narrow-mindedness, and many of our people need it sorely on these accounts."[1] It would be nice to think that short-term mission trips produce broad-minded global citizens and deal fatal blows to our bigoted ethnocentrism. But Mark Twain was never on a short-term mission trip, and I've seen plenty of "our people" who "need it sorely" return from such trips with their prejudices and ethnocentrism not only alive but bolstered. Their prejudice leaks out in comments like, "I realized how blessed we are to be in America," or in the sweeping generalizations made from someone who has less experience in a host country than the two-year old child they played with in the vacation Bible school their church hosted.

One must wonder, though, if even Mark Twain believed that travel alone would spawn broad-mindedness and kill prejudice. In his book *American Vandal: Mark Twain Abroad*, Roy Morris describes the American traveler in Twain's book, this way: "A brazen, unapologetic visitor to foreign

---

1. Twain, *Innocents Abroad*, 685.

132

lands, generally unimpressed with the local ambiance—to say nothing of the local inhabitants—but ever ready to appropriate any religious or historical trinket he or she could carry off."[2]

What we're talking about with many short-term mission programs is a form of tourism—and tourism grew out of the soil of colonization. The primary beneficiary is the tourist, for whom the experience is about personal aggrandizement. True, tourism, like short-term mission trips, infuses cash into the places they visit, but often at the expense of the environment and with a measure of objectifying the local cultures and people. International travel is available, by and large, only to those with an excess of time and money. It is a form of cultural vandalism for the sake of personal education or pleasure.

Sometimes short-term mission trips fashion us into anthropologists, and while anthropology has increased our understanding and appreciation of humanity across cultures, its origins are also located in the effort to colonize. We study a people, not so much to contribute to the well-being of their society, but to add to our knowledge base. Empires can then leverage this knowledge toward its own expansion, whether academically, politically or economically. Those of us who live in imperial countries like America need to understand that our learning-focused mission trips are colored by our anthropological, colonizing past. The exploitative impulse in tourism and anthropology may be unconsciously shaping the mindset of the well-meaning international traveler.

This doesn't mean that we should never give in to curiosity about people, their cultures, their foods, their monuments and their history. Our world is too beautiful and diverse to remain cloistered in our homogenous enclaves. Let's get out there, but in ways that contribute more to the equation than simply our personal learning and our money. Adding cash to an economy through our room, board, and travel dollars (not all of which remain in that country or go to local residents) for the sake of our self-actualization is just paying to vandalize a culture. Travelers have more to offer than money. Things like solidarity, listening to others's stories, and setting mutual learning outcomes for both visitor and host, move us from the one-way transactions that often define these trips.

2. Morris, *American Vandal*, 7

Trips Accessible to All

If we want to disrupt the unhealthy dynamics that characterize STM practices, a good place to begin is by asking who gets to go on these trips in the first place. When a trip is available almost exclusively to those with wealth (or those with access to people with wealth who might donate money), we have already set up a dangerous dynamic. The wealth of the world has not been fairly dispersed. Money continues to accumulate into the hands of fewer and fewer people, leaving many people who are rich in character stuck in cycles of generational poverty. Short-term mission trips too often exaggerate the income gap between traveler and host, simply by virtue of the cost of travel and availability of free time. But for these trips to be accessible mainly to the middle class or rich means that the teams themselves become class-based echo-chambers, robbing participants of the power that comes when those from well-resourced backgrounds and those from poorly resourced backgrounds live and serve side-by-side.

I (Scott) remember being with a team in a province in China where an oppressed minority is the majority population. Our team included participants from lower economic backgrounds who were able to join because those of us with access to wealth carried a larger share of the cost of the trip. Those from American ethnic minority backgrounds (many of whom suffer generational economic exclusion) opened relational doors with the Chinese minority participants and advanced the learning of all as majority culture and minority culture compared life experiences in both countries. It was our economic diversity that made the trip valuable and grew deep bonds through challenging conversations.

One strategy then that works against short-term teams becoming a class-based vandal horde is to craft the economics of a trip so that it is accessible to participants of all economic backgrounds. People without financial resources have things to contribute as well as things to learn, so trip pricing should address the economic disparities that exist in a given country.

Put Away Your Wallet

CRAIG GREENFIELD

AFTER MANY YEARS LIVING in Cambodian slums, I have seen a lot of harm done by well-meaning do-gooders with money. I have made many of these mistakes myself. Too often, we arrive with our western mindset that applies an economic solution to every problem. And we overwhelm the local community with our vast resources. Local people may be more than happy to receive your money. However, let's consider the following:

What Happens When the Money Gets Cut Off?

As eleven thousand NGO's found in India after a government crackdown, everything grinds to a halt when outside funds stop.[3] Entire organizations had to shut down because they couldn't continue without outside funding. Money is not wrong in and of itself. It can be used to create ongoing sustainability, or it can be used to create dependency. The problem arises when money becomes the main foundation of our ministry. When it is removed, the ministry collapses. Local people must be central to God's work of transformation in any healthy ministry. And we must be careful of any ministry that relies too heavily on short-term volunteers from outside; it may be unsustainable. And the sad fact is that often these types of projects are designed around regularly welcoming short-term teams, in great part because those teams bring money.

Money Distorts the Relationship between the Wisdom of an Idea and the Results

Anything can happen—even the dumbest, most disempowering idea—simply because money is paid to ensure it happens. There

3. Barry and Raj, "Major Christian Charity Is Closing India Operations Amid a Crackdown," https://www.nytimes.com/2017/03/07/world/asia/compassion-international-christian-charity-closing-india.html.

will always be impoverished people willing to carry out a foreigner's misguided project just because they receive a salary. But the true test of an idea is whether people are willing to embrace it without getting paid.

Money Concentrates Power in the Hands of Donors and Those with Access to Funding, Instead of the Poor and Vulnerable

There is a significant role for donors and funding. After all, almost everything costs something. But they must serve from the periphery, not call the shots. Everyone agrees with that statement in theory, but it's very hard to practice. That's why money-fueled growth is so dangerous—and so common. Clarence Jordan said, "What the poor need is not charity but capital, not caseworkers but coworkers. And what the rich need is a wise, honorable and just way of divesting themselves of their overabundance." [4]

The Use of Money for Change Can't Be Easily Replicated by Local People

A church plant funded by outside money will likely have great difficulty birthing another church without the same cash injection. The same goes for any other project or initiative. When we model methods of transformation that can't be replicated, we ourselves become the main and only drivers of change—once again marginalizing the poor to whom such initiatives ought to belong.

The unwise use of cash is just one example of how we tend to pursue transformation—with good intentions but bad strategies. There are many more damaging shortcuts that can make our efforts do more harm than good: using corruption or manipulation, cutting corners, exaggerating in our marketing, exploiting our beneficiaries and their stories, using outside power and force rather than taking the time to empower local leaders, and so on.

4. Habitat for Humanity, "Koinonia Farm and the Fund for Humanity."

Yes, we are called to pursue good—but we must do that according to the timing and guidance of God, as well as proven strategies—not using methods driven by our own impatience. As Brian Zhand says: "Satan never tempted Jesus with evil; Satan tempted Jesus with good. Satan enticed Jesus to go ahead and do good and to bring it about by the most direct way possible."[5]

It's easy to kid ourselves with the lie that the end justifies the means. That it doesn't matter how we achieve our good goals, as long as people are "helped." But this isn't true. The lesson I take from the temptation of Jesus is this: the end never justifies the means. Funding is definitely needed. Redistribution of resources from the wealthy to the poor is an important biblical practice. But these things are not easily navigated while on a brief visit. He is inviting us to take the long view, the sustainable road, the best pathway. And in doing so, we trust that God's upside-down kingdom will come; to do otherwise is to build our own.

Craig Greenfield

Craig Greenfield is the founder of Alongsiders International, a grassroots discipleship movement of eight thousand children and youth across Asia and Africa. He is the author of *Subversive Jesus* and the upcoming book, *Outsider Calling*. Visit his blog at www.craiggreenfield.com.

Bibliography

Barry, E., and Raj, S. "Major Christian Charity is Closing India Operations Amid a Crackdown." *The New York Times* (2017).

Habitat for Humanity, "Koinonia Farm and the Fund for Humanity." *Habitat For Humanity* (2021).

Zahnd, Brian. *Beauty Will Save the World: Rediscovering the Allure and Mystery of Christianity.* Lake Mary, FL: Charisma House, 2012.

5. Zahnd, *Beauty Will Save the World*, 20.

Collaborative Learning Objectives
for Both Host and Guest

When learning is primarily focused on the education of the visitor, we have become vandals, exploiting our hosts for our personal educational purposes. One important way to encourage mutuality of learning is to have an equal number of local participants and visitors, and then for visitors and hosts to co-create the learning outcomes. Both have something to teach and something to learn, and each will have a different perspective on just how to achieve those goals. This may be done ahead of time by leaders, but room should be made for the participants themselves to help define the experience. Locals and visitors should make sure that teacher and student roles switch regularly throughout a trip.

I (Scott) have a Mexican friend who created an organization which served marginalized communities and often hosted large groups of North Americans on service-learning trips. His organization ran a number of guest houses to accommodate these groups. We decided to set up a trip which included the housekeeping staff from these guest houses as full-on participants. On the first day the Americans and Mexicans defined the sort of learning we each wanted to experience from the trip. Mexican maids, along with their children, and foreign Americans each grew from the experience because each had a chance to voice what they wanted to learn.

Reciprocal Learning in Action

I (Ben) spent more than thirty years living among the dumpsite scavengers of Smokey Mountain in Manila, Philippines. During that time, American InterVarsity students stayed with the scavengers in Smokey Mountain, living among families and helping with the kindergarten established there. In the five consecutive years of visits, they taught lessons to school dropouts and joined in Bible studies led by Pilipino Christians, hearing scriptural insights offered by those living and working in the garbage dump. American students who studied IT helped to digitize modules for the computer-based learning of the school dropouts and gave lessons in english, science and math. Those who studied management helped in the use of cellphones and text messaging for an e-trading network. The Americans also went on excursions with Pilipino kids to the markets and food stalls in the area and swam with them at the beaches away from the hustle and bustle of Metro Manila. All in all, we benefited greatly from these yearly visits.

Of course, the sharing of time and talents went both ways! The youth from Smokey Mountain formed a traditional Pilipino dance group and were brought to the United States by the InterVarsity students that had stayed with them in the garbage dump. As those who experience climate change most acutely (as do many living in poverty) they were given a United States platform to proclaim their message of care for creation: to wound the earth is to wound ourselves. The dancers stayed with the families of the InterVarsity students, and it was a powerful reciprocating experience for both groups. The Pilipino youth went with the Americans to a Golden State Warriors basketball game, visited the Golden Gate Bridge and rode the ferry. After this they buckled down to rehearse for their environmental concerts, calling attention to the dangers of climate change through their dances, and warning us that the human race might suffer untold misery if we continue to ravage the earth and remain blind to the plight of the poor. In addition, the American team members also brought me to three student missions conferences to talk about ecological issues among dumpsite scavengers, and the need to work together to assure future generations enter a sustainable future.

As you can see, it is possible to shape STM trips so that they are less one-sided. The American InterVarsity group came to Manila for five years running, helping out in the garbage dump and participating in the spiritual, educational and economic dimensions of life. I often asked the American students about their experience, and they would say that their faith was strengthened by the experience of the Smokey Mountain community praying earnestly and trusting God in the midst of life on the trash heaps.

This is simply one example of how reciprocal STM experiences do exist and serve as a better way forward. There are none so rich that they have nothing to learn, and none so poor that they have nothing to give, even the destitute scavengers of the garbage dump called Smokey Mountain in the heart of Manila, Philippines.

Ripples That Move Outward

When there is no plan for our learning to ripple outward to others, we play into the glorification of the self that is so prevalent in hyper-individualistic cultures. We become consumers, checking off the list of countries we've been to, foods we've tried, or bucket-list items we've accomplished. Our photos and souvenirs become the booty of our raids, inflating our egos and proving just how cosmopolitan, well-learned, and generous we are.

But egos are tyrannical masters, demanding that all stories point back to us as the hero. And any self-deprecation serves only to accentuate our heroic humility. But there are ways to ensure our travel has a centrifugal force, spinning benefits outward to others while at the same time growing our own worldview from the trip. We need to arrange our trips in such a way as to plan for ongoing relationships with one or two of the people we meet. Even if the ongoing relationship is for a limited period of time, our experience will become a set of living relationships rather than just an album of static photos and a t-shirt.

I (Scott) have seen trips set up so that they include sponsoring our new friends from abroad to come visit us in the following year, similar to Father Ben's example of the reciprocal trip between the InterVarsity students and the dance group of the Smokey Mountain. Again, this may require some kind of built-in redistribution of wealth—yet in ways that avoid making a patron out of the person who happened to be born on the wealthier side of the global economic divide, and a client of the one born on the economic margins.

The benefits of an international trip should have ripple effects that go both inward to the traveler and outward to the community. When Paul and Barnabas returned to Antioch from the first missionary journey, they gathered the church and reported "how he had opened a door of faith to the Gentiles."[6] They were careful to push their learning outward to their home community and communicate stories about God's work in and among the Gentiles.

It is time for western-spawned short-term mission trips to experience a redesign, departing from our colonizing past that pushes us toward vandalizing other people and places for our own expansion. We might begin by making sure our trips are not accessible just to those from middle-class and wealthy backgrounds. We ought also to consider establishing cocreated learning outcomes with our hosts abroad. And then become a centrifugal force, so that those who travel and those who host can all enjoy and steward the learning, not only for themselves but for those around them. A truly fundamental redesign of short-term trips requires a whole new way of thinking about ourselves, about God, and about the world.

6. Acts 14:27 (ESV).

Scott Bessenecker

Scott Bessenecker is Director of Global Engagement and Justice for Inter-Varsity Christian Fellowship. He oversees InterVarsity's holistic mission through their Global Programs, Justice Programs and Study Abroad. Scott is author or editor of five books, including *The New Friars* and *Overturning Tables*. He hosts a blog and a few podcasts on his website www.overturning-tables.com. He lives in Madison, Wisconsin, with his wife Janine who is a watercolor artist, and has three grown children, Hannah, Philip, and Laura.

Fr. Benigno Beltran

Fr. Ben studied Electronics Engineering at University of Santo Tomas, before joining the Divine Word Missionaries. He was ordained on June, 23 1973 and received his Licentiate and Doctorate in Systematic Theology at the Pontifical University of the Gregorian. Fr. Ben was the pastor of scavengers in a garbage dump called Smokey Mountain in the heart of Manila from 1978–2008. During that time, he also taught theology at the Divine Word Seminary, Tagaytay City. He is now engaged in the use of cloud technologies to educate out-of-school youth so that they can proceed to college, engage in entrepreneurial activities, or gain employment.

Bibliography

Twain, Mark. *The Innocents Abroad.* New York City: Chelsea House, 2021.
Morris, Roy. *American Vandal. Mark Twain Abroad.* Cambridge, MA: Belknap, 2015.

12

Candy Machine Charity

Bonita Broadnax *and* Brian Fikkert,
with Emily Carminati

There's something really strange about how the western church does short-term missions. Most of us have probably been part of it without realizing just how weird it is. Of course, this is an audacious claim, but let us offer two anecdotes—true stories that may feel very familiar to those who have participated in short-term missions.

I (Bonita) serve as the manager of a Section 8 housing complex in Chattanooga, Tennessee, with more than its share of violence and poverty. Some time ago, I began reaching out to local churches to invite them to come and partner with my complex and bring the love of God to those living under my care in this community. One church finally took me up on the idea and expressed excitement about building relationships and bringing the hope of Christ to our community. And they proposed a plan: they would pitch a tent, and bring food and Christian rap music to make community members feel comfortable. The day came; the church's outreach team members piled out of cars and set up the tent. They put out a table with water and snacks, set up a portable speaker, and turned on the music. We prayed together, then I left them to begin their ministry. One member of the team went out from the tent, walked through the property, greeted residents, engaged in brief conversation, and returned to the tent. The remaining team members never left the tent or took time to have meaningful conversations with any of the residents. After they packed up and went home, needless to say, no one had been "saved." No one had been prayed with. No one had even eaten the snacks!

The second story features a short-term team that traveled from three hours away to do service work in the housing complex. They brought their own painting supplies, and worked six-hour days painting the stair railings in every building in the complex. They seemed comfortable in this setting, and were friendly and warm to the residents. Yet they were intent on their work, and even though they worked in close proximity to the community residents, they kept conversations short and shallow. When that team had gone, all the painting was complete—and that was certainly a gift to our community. But were any lives changed? Were any real relationships formed? Sadly, the beautiful paint jobs were the only lasting sign of that team's presence.

In both of these stories, we witness one of the profound oddities of conventional short-term missions thinking: in the name of sharing love and saving people's souls, people are nevertheless treated as objects; there is an uncritical assumption that technique and strategy yields personally transformative results among the targets of STM efforts. Snacks, rap music, even service projects and small talk—these are not bad things in themselves, but they don't actually do anything to meet the basic need of humans with souls: that is, relationship.

The weirdness of this objectifying model of short-term ministry becomes clearer if we flip the script and try to see the situation from the stance of the community (rather than inside the tent). Think about it: if someone from another cultural or religious persuasion pitched a tent in front of your house, put out snacks and drinks, and expected you to show curiosity about their beliefs—or much less, to win you over to their religion—would you even go near them? It would be impossible to interpret their actions as anything like love or authentic relationship. If anything, you might feel like these strangers to the neighborhood saw you as a target, a task, or a potential conquest.

At its core, this problem of western missions is a theological and anthropological one. I (Brian) discuss this in my book, *Becoming Whole*. There is a tendency in western anthropology to reduce the human being merely to a physical, material creature and to overlook the presence of a soul. If we think the human being is just a physical creature, we can treat our interactions with them like using a candy machine—put a quarter in and something sweet pops out. We engage them in purely material terms. For Christians, there's a tendency to simply tack on concern for the soul to this framework, without reevaluating the overall approach. So, we pitch the tent, fill it with Bibles and tracts, blast Christian rap, and assume that if we only flash enough "Truth," the objects of our efforts might somehow get their souls "saved." And we keep on repeating strategies like this without acknowledging the fact that they rarely get anyone saved, and might even be driving people further away from any engagement with the real truth of the gospel. The "problem" with many of our short-term mission approaches is that humans are not just physical bodies with souls tacked on, and nor are they anything like candy machines; rather, they are created for authentic relationship, and desperately in need of the love of a relational God.

If the core purpose of short-term missions, service projects, and outreach trips is to draw people into a loving relationship with God, we have to remember (and perhaps re-learn) what love actually looks like. And if we flip the tent-missions paradigm around once again and consider how *we* would like to be loved—to have love shared with us—it would certainly not look like someone pitching a tent in our neighborhood and putting on a circus. Rather, love that might elicit a response could only be communicated by those who take the time to know us and care about us, with no ulterior motives or agendas—just simple, authentic relationships for relationship's sake. Unfortunately, the likelihood of a church outreach team or missions group being able to build authentic relationships, locally or internationally, within the time limits of a typical short-term missions trip, service project, or outreach day is very low indeed. Authentic relationship doesn't grow in a mere forty-five minutes, nor in three days, nor even in three weeks.

What, then, can a short-term team do to bring the love of God to a Section 8 housing complex in their city—or to a village on the other side of the world? First and foremost, they can support the workers who are already there. They can come alongside the long-term missionaries, the indigenous pastors, or the Section 8 housing complex managers who are already doing the slow, patient, love-work of building relationships. *These* are the people who are living as the hands and feet of Christ—in ways that short-term outsiders (no matter their good intentions) cannot. These people are going to be around for the long haul, to share meals together, to be present for community celebrations and losses, to meet complex needs. Yet while short-term teams cannot love people in those same ways, they *can* get behind the men and women who do, supporting them financially, physically, socially, and spiritually. Short-term teams must not only seek to support the work of those who serve long-term—they must also be guided by them in any service activities for the larger community.

We began with two anecdotes of short-term missions gone wrong. Let us end with an example of missions done well. There is one local church that has been showing up at the housing complex for *twenty-six years.* When they come, they come for several weeks at a time. *In everything they do, they serve the long-term goals of the community's leaders, and submit themselves to the wisdom of those who are there every day.* At the same time, the visiting team members prioritize spending time with people, setting aside transactional evangelism strategies. For those reasons, residents of the housing complex have come to trust this church. They count on the resources the team brings to share, and eagerly anticipate the programs the team sponsors. While the residents may not know every visitor's name, they do know that they will be seen and treated like real people when this church comes to be with them. That is because the visiting church members have taken time over many years to build relationships, to become familiar faces, to stick around long enough to experience at least a little bit of what life is like in the community. To the community members, this church's presence never looks weird; rather, it looks like love.

Bonita Broadnax

Bonita Broadnax is a former Section 8 property manager for a private affordable housing company in Chattanooga, TN. Prior to property management, she served as an AmeriCorps VISTA focused on alleviating poverty at a Chattanooga-based affordable housing nonprofit. Ms. Broadnax holds a master's in International Community Development and has over twenty-five years of experience in cultural studies, inclusion and equity practices, and actionable solutions to complex social issues.

Brian Fikkert

Dr. Brian Fikkert is the Founder and President of the Chalmers Center for Economic Development at Covenant College (www.chalmers.org) where he also serves as a Professor of Economics and Community Development. Brian has published articles in both leading academic and popular journals and has co-authored numerous books including *Becoming Whole: Why the Opposite of Poverty isn't the American Dream* (Moody 2019); *Helping Without Hurting in Short-Term Missions* (Moody 2014); *When Helping Hurts: How to Alleviate Poverty without Hurting the Poor . . . and Yourself* (Moody 2009).

Emily Carminati

Emily is a communications expert, community development practitioner, and writer working in an international ministry setting. She finds many ways to combine her passions for cross-cultural learning, telling stories in ways that honor, and building copowering partnerships that lead to transformation. Emily lives with her two children and her husband in Oregon.

13

Rethinking (the Social Imaginary of) Short-Term Missions

Brian Howell

In 2001, I started teaching at Wheaton College, a Christian liberal arts school outside Chicago. I would often start my Introduction to Anthropology classes by asking students about any experiences they had outside their home culture. At previous teaching jobs, my students would talk about a trip across the Canadian border, a Caribbean cruise, or perhaps a neighborhood they had visited in the United States with a diverse population. Occasionally, I would have students with little experience. One woman could only think of one example, eating at a Chinese restaurant. But Wheaton students were different.[1] In addition to my international students, and missionary kids, I had many students who had traveled to such places as urban South Africa, highland Guatemala, Northern Ghana, and villages in the Wales countryside. They had done service work, painted churches, led

---

1. It's important to note that my previous teaching gigs were also mostly working-class, non-traditional students. Wheaton College is almost entirely students in the eighteen to twenty-two year range, and vastly over-represent the top 20% of incomes in the United States.

soccer camps, and taught English. It was somewhat surprising to me, not only the extent of their travels, but the high percentage of students who had such stories. They had all been on a short-term mission trip.

What was most striking to me about my students and their experiences, however, was not the simple fact that such a high percentage were participating, or the wide variety of their travels, but how they spoke about these trips. Common phrases such as "it was a life-changing experience," "the people were so poor, but so happy," "I received more than I gave," were peppered throughout a narrative that frequently almost mirrored the conversion narrative common in Christian life. Once I was blind, but now I see.

This led me to question where this narrative came from, how it became so regularized, and to ask what effect it could have on the ways people experience and process these trips throughout their lives.[2] For my research, I first spent a summer with my family in the place in the Dominican Republic where I knew a short-term missions team would be going the following summer. Then I spent time with that team, participating in the process of preparing for our trip, and then traveled with the team the following summer. I was able to both interview people about their experiences and expectations, as well as observe the everyday work of preparing, thinking, narrating, and developing an understanding of STM among this group.

The primary question—the same question of this volume—I have continued to think about is not just the ways we directly create these narratives, but the raw materials we work with. Whether here at Wheaton, or just in my church life, my research has sensitized me to the ways we (re)create narratives of mission, travel, "the exotic," and our sense of "calling" to construct these narratives of STM. I remain convinced that the narratives we foster have a profound impact on the ways these trips shape both the participants who travel as well as the communities that receive them.

As Cyrius et al. argue, every narrative has characters, a setting, and a plot.[3] The narratives that emerged from the preparation of my team traveling to the Dominican Republic had a strong and specific shape that often served to inhibit our understanding of some of the very things we set out to learn. It was a narrative of "mission" that emerged within this specific context of this congregation, reflecting this specific history and social context. At the same time, this narrative provided the means for us to make sense of our

2. This is the central question in my book, *Short Term Mission: an Ethnography of Christian Travel Narrative and Experience.*

3. See Cyrius et al., observations in chapter 5 of this volume, 53–66.

experiences. Coming from a highly individualist context, in which the trip was framed as a "life changing" experience, we created a narrative about personal transformation and individual relationships that both linked our trip to a theological framework and served to obscure aspects of the very things our team wanted to understand: poverty, inequality, and cultural difference.

Since doing that research more than ten years ago, I have seen even more clearly how the narrative that emerged prior to the trip was strongly shaped by the much wider cultural context. That is, our narratives were not just formed at the church or by one another; they came from the world around us. These narratives were constructed out of the images, phrases, and associations we carried from the wider world.

For the past eight years, then, I have been very aware of the kinds of images and phrases that tend to get associated with STM and how they shape our thinking about these efforts. Judging by those with whom I interact as I continue to speak and write on STM, there is greater awareness of some of these more problematic images or phrases. At the same time, there are still many that need to be identified, if not problematized, in their association with STM. As we become more aware of how particular phrases, words, and images carry forward into STM narratives, we will be better equipped to change the narratives that are shaping our ability to live out the *missio Dei* in all that we do.

In this chapter, I will briefly summarize the work I did ten years ago in understanding STM and the concepts of narrative and social imaginary I used for that work. Then, I will look at a couple phrases, terms, and images that often show up in relation to STM. Looking at some of the cultural material we use in creating our ideas of STM, I suggest how we might become more critically engaged with our culture in order to resist the forming of our minds in patterns that do not serve the kingdom work we're called to do. I don't intend these as representative or "trends," but rather as examples that will serve to help anyone thinking about this topic to become more equipped to identify and interrogate such cultural symbols for themselves. In order to avoid the sense that I am attacking the STM enterprise, I draw on both positive and problematic examples to make the points. Ultimately, I argue that only when we become more adept at reading the symbols around us—exegeting the culture, as it were—will we be able to effectively transform our thinking in gospel centered ways.

Narratives, Social Imaginaries, and the Creation of Meaning

The focus on narratives in social theory is popular—trendy even—but it is not new. Contemporary philosopher Michel de Certeau put *narrative* at the heart of his theory of human action and interpretation. He argued that "the story does not express a practice. It does not limit itself to telling about a movement. It *makes* it."[4] But his ideas were not revolutionary. Rather, he reaches back into the eighteenth century work of Sigmund Freud, the seventeenth century thinking of Immanuel Kant, and back into the work of Aristotle and the dramatists of ancient Greece. The power of stories in shaping human life have been around a long time. Today, the emphasis on narrative as a foundation of human life and behavior can be seen in the work of such thinkers as philosopher Charles Taylor and theologian James K.A. Smith. What they have done, however, is expand our understanding of these narratives to include more than words that form plots, scenes, and characters. Rather, they argue that humans don't rely on just a system of coherent beliefs to understand the world; instead we use a collection of images, story fragments, and plot points as we confront every new thing in the world. Thus, these scholars foreground what they call the "social imaginary." The social imaginary, writes Taylor, is "not a set of ideas; rather, it is what enables, through making sense of, the practices of a society."[5] It is the images, associations, and tropes that we draw from to make sense of ourselves, our experiences, and our memories in the narratives we create.

This has been particularly helpful for scholars of tourism where travelers often encounter a panoply—a kaleidescope! A carnival (perhaps literally!)—of new people, sounds, smells, language, practices, tastes, and differences of all kinds. For any human being entering such an array of unfamiliar life, he or she must sort it out into categories and patterns that make sense. They (often unconsciously) draw on the images and ideas to which they have previously been exposed to make sense of the newness. Anthropologists Noel Salazar and Nelson Graburn called these "tourist imaginaries."[6] That is, when travelers set out to a new place they have never been, they still have images of what they expect to find and why this is an interesting place to go; and they may be disappointed if they don't see it as

---

4. Certeau, *Practice of Everyday Life*, 81.

5. Taylor, *Modern Social Imaginaries*, 1.

6. Salazar, *Tourism Imaginaries*, 1.

it appeared in their mind's eye, even as they seek out those things that they most associate with the place or people they've come to visit. For example, for most white North Americans, "Africa" stands in with images of a rolling savanna where wildebeest, lions, and colorful Maasai herdsmen who exist in a Circle of Life.[7] On the other hand, any tropical beach in almost any part of the world can serve as an imagined place of "paradise:" leisure, pleasure, and an almost time-less carefree life.[8] And in the tourist encounter, both those hosting the tourists and the tourists themselves, employ their social imaginaries of the others they encounter to inform how they should act and treat these new partners encountered through tourist travels.[9]

These social imaginaries then provide the raw materials for the stories we tell ourselves about what we're experiencing, as well as how we plan to remember and recount these experiences to others. I saw this in my own research as I watched that group of high school students from Wheaton, IL encounter the Dominican Republic through their social imagination. During one two-week mission trip to the island nation, I joined a small group of these students during some free time as we walked from the house where our team was staying in a quiet, middle-class neighborhood in a picturesque mountain town. Several of the boys in the group were in search of gifts to bring home to friends and siblings, and one had in mind the perfect thing, a 'machete.' As we walked, looking in the tourist-oriented shops for the sort of large blade he had in mind, he talked about why it seemed the perfect gift. "I'm just thinking I want something that is, like, the jungle, you know? Just when I picture the D.R., I think of cutting away in the jungle. You know what I mean?" We looked in a number of shops, with no luck. We asked some of the shop keepers, stringing together our Spanish, and having very little luck with the word *machete*. Finally, one man figured out that we meant what is locally known as a *bolo*, and sent us up the street . . . to the hardware store. Dominicans selling to tourists had not, at that time, anticipated this image of their country as one of "jungles" and bushwacking through tropical undergrowth, or the determination of my young friend to find this object that, to him, captured his vision of this tropical island. Despite the fact that we had not (and would not) have occasion to go into any sort of natural preserve in which cutting through "the jungle" would be necessary, this association of this Caribbean nation with a vision of an

7. Bruner, "Maasai and the Lion King," 208–36.

8. See for example, Lüfgren, *Holiday: A History of Vacationing.*

9. Stasch, "Symmetric Treatment of Imaginaries," 31–57.

Amazonian-style jungle adventure was strong. He bought three of the *bolo* knives from a somewhat bemused shopkeeper at the hardware store, who surely must have thought it curious that this tourist would buy garden tools while visiting his country.

This is, in one sense, a trivial example. This young man was a kind and thoughtful participant in the STM. He treated people with compassion, and was an eager learner. But it illustrates the point of how our perceptions of a place may be formed less by the actual location or people, and more by our imagination of that place. I can certainly imagine how popular images of the tropical rain forest from films like *The Jungle Book*, or cultural tropes adapted by television shows like *Survivor* or *Naked and Afraid* help to keep such associations alive. I am sure he had no explicitly negative stereotypes in mind as he imagined the DR as the untamed jungle, yet the very word "jungle" has associations with chaos and primitivity ("Be careful! It's a jungle out there!")[10] The idea of this nation as a jungle is easily connected to our explicit intention to engage poverty in this "underdeveloped" nation. The jungle imaginary brings all these together, symbolized in the souvenir machete.

These sorts of imaginaries often go unexamined as they just seem obvious or "common sense." Yet they are not natural; they are created in the cultural worlds from which we come. These are not "worldviews" or explicit, systemic beliefs about the people or places we visit. The young man on our team knew we would be staying in an urban area and could see, as well as I, that there weren't any jungles in the vicinity. He didn't *believe* the DR was a jungle nation. It just *felt* like one. The idea of the DR just seemed . . . well . . . jungle-y.

So, the questions can be asked: what are the other ideas, words, images, and feelings we have around STM? How might those terms center the STM travelers in a narrative in which they should be smaller players in a story centered on the host communities? By identifying some of those that seem common, and exploring how they might be questioned, we can do a better job of constructing narratives of STM that serve the best ideals and theology of what these trips could be.

---

10. Tourism scholars have long noted the association of the "jungle" with images of the "primitive" and "remote" undeveloped lands in the imagination of western travelers. See, for example, Cohen, "Primitive and Remote: Hill Tribe Trekking in Thailand."

Imaginary Partnerships

In the past ten years, one of the shifts in STM that I have seen is the development in "church to church partnerships." These are relationships established between two congregations, or denominational units (dioceses or districts or regions) in which groups develop long-term relationships. These are, in many cases, explicitly developed to counteract a concern that STM trips can be disruptive, superficial, or even neocolonialist in their execution without some kind of relationship that continues beyond the two weeks. Certainly, much of the research on STM points to the creation of what is known as "linking capital," or the establishment of relationships whereby resources (human, material, or social) can be transferred from one context to another through the establishment of these social ties.[11] A quick look at a number of STM organizations reveals that many employ "partners" or "partnership" in their name.[12]

The point here is not to suggest that using the term "partner" or "partnership" is *necessarily* problematic in itself. As Cyrius, et al. demonstrate, partnerships that involve financial and administrative sharing can bring real and lasting shifts in patterns of multinational work.[13] Yet, the word *partnership* itself can also serve as part of a social imagination that gives the appearance of mutuality, yet without substance. In order to distinguish the veneer of partnership from its reality, then, we should be prepared to interrogate the word. To start, we must ask ourselves: what images and feelings does the term "partnership" bring to mind?

Surely, part of the appeal of the word is the notion of equality. A "partner" is often a peer, colleague, or even romantic or marital relation with whom a person has a life-long commitment. Partnerships might be symbolized by a handshake, a hug, or another sign of friendship. "Partnership" may bring to mind a business relationship; two people or groups working together toward a common goal. It's certainly a friendly, if a bit socially-distanced word. For someone who has grown up in the United States, and perhaps is a certain age, the term "partner" might bring up the image of a cowboy riding up on his horse, and greeting someone he may or may

---

11. Priest, "Short-Term Missions as a New Paradigm," 84–100.

12. The organizations on ShortTermMissions.org include "Global Partnership Ministries," "e3 Partners," and "Utah Partnerships for Christ."

13. See Cyrius et al. observations in chapter 5 of this volume, 53–66.

not know with a friendly, "Howdy, partner." Partners are pairs, friends, and likely equals working out their relationship and common goals.

Given these associations—the way "partnership" invokes a particular social imaginary—what this term may obscure in a STM trip are the power imbalances that often, even usually, cohere in these relationships. Those receiving an STM team from a (generally) wealthier, more politically powerful place have more at risk if an STM team is unhappy. As Steve Offut has noted in his study of STM hosts in South Africa, the hosts are often working very hard to anticipate what the visitors want, and trying to provide it.[14] They are not necessarily thinking about their own ministry and what they *need*, because one of the most widespread needs is for resources—resources they hope this relationship with relatively wealthy Christian visitors might provide. This is not to say that hosts are all mercenary, and visitors all manipulators. Far from it. In my time in the Dominican Republic, virtually every Dominican with whom I spoke was very glad for STM visitors, including those who stood to gain very little in terms of economic or even social capital. Rather they were glad the team would spend time in their community; they appreciated the chance to show them their lives. But they were also *quite* aware of the imbalance of power in the relationship. They did not, for the most part, speak of these teams as their "partners." In her book *Cross-Cultural Partnerships: Navigating the Complexities of Missions and Money*, Mary Lederleitner relates the comment of an Anglican bishop in Tanzania who told the North American Wycliffe area director that, "You are too powerful to be good partners."[15] The director understood this to mean not that they could not have a partnership, but that it would take a great deal of work to overcome the power differential and be *good* partners.

Equality is not something produced by intention, conviction, or moral assertion alone. While a commitment to equality is a necessary condition for partnership, it is certainly not sufficient. Again, as the example from Konbit Haiti demonstrates, for a partnership to create the conditions for mutual flourishing that God desires, the partners must attend to the economic, administrative, and social power at work. If the (usually less resourced) host country is asked for input without giving them meaningful access or control over material resources, they are unlikely to suggest activities that may be less pleasing to the visitors, (regardless of the actual needs of the work) or risk giving the kind of critical advice the visitors may need.

14. Offutt, "Role of Short-Term Mission Teams," 796.
15. Lederleitner, *Cross-Cultural Partnerships*, 121–22.

Partnership is a culturally embedded term that evokes a range of images and associations, but it is never merely descriptive. It is a moral and ethical term. It has a history and even a theology. It must be interrogated if we are to see past what this term evokes in our social imaginary, to see what is actually present in our relationships across cultural, economic, and political lines. It may be wiser, as several chapters in this volume suggest, to create new terms, such as "copowerment," to produce the kind of social imagination that can reveal the material, social, and spiritual dimensions of relationships in a way that encourages mutuality in ways that terms like "partnership" may obscure.

In her article, "When the Elephant Dances, Mouse May Die," anthropologist and missiologist Miriam Adeney recounts this story told to her by a West African ministry leader to suggest how the "partnership" of wealthy STM visitors and hosts often proceeds. She writes:

> "Would you like to know what it is like to do mission with Americans? Let me tell you a story," said David Coulibaly, a ministry leader in Mali, West Africa.
>
> Elephant and Mouse were best friends. One day Elephant said, "Mouse, let's have a party!"
>
> Animals gathered from far and near. They ate, and drank, and sang, and danced. And nobody celebrated more exuberantly than Elephant.
>
> After it was over, Elephant exclaimed, "Mouse, did you ever go to a better party? What a blast!"
>
> But Mouse didn't answer.
>
> "Where are you?" Elephant called. Then he shrank back in horror. There at his feet lay the mouse, his body ground into the dirt—smashed by the exuberance of his friend, Elephant.
>
> "Sometimes that is what it is like to do mission with you Americans," the African storyteller concluded. "It is like dancing with an elephant."[16]

---

16. Adeney, "When the Elephant Dances," 156–60.

Images of Adventure

Another term that is common in STM is the term "adventure." The word "adventure" is front and center in the name of some STM organizations. There is an STM guide from 2006 entitled *Equipped for Adventure: A Practical Guide to Short-Term Mission.*[17] The term adventure is *widely* used in STM promotions, often coupled with such phrases as "life-change experience" and "world changing."

It's not difficult to see why this word resonates for many North American STM travelers. For a person who may have never traveled internationally, never been in a low-income community, never been in the racial minority, or immersed in a non-English-speaking context, there is no doubt that the trip would be exciting. In short, it would be what many of us would call an adventure.

But, like the term partnership, *adventure* carries many associations and connotations that contribute to a specific social imaginary. It isn't hard, for example, to connect "adventure" with "danger," "bravery," and "heroism." *The Adventures of Indiana Jones* and *The Adventures of Robin Hood* chronicle men who fearlessly rush into danger to rescue people (and gold statues) from threatening situations. *Adventure* brings to mind exotic (meaning non-western, often non-white) locations. The entry for "Adventure Films" in Wikipedia reads simply "a genre of film that typically use their action scenes to display and explore exotic locations in an energetic way."[18] It goes on to identify "pirate films" and "survivor films" as subgenres of the adventure film.

Like my young teammate and his image of the "jungle" of the Dominican Republic, identifying one's STM trip as an "adventure" is a small piece of an overall experience a person has; I don't mean to suggest that organizations using the notion of "adventure" are irreparably wounding their teams in their ability to engage humbly, thoughtfully, and appropriately. But I would argue that calling such a trip "an adventure" doesn't help. It supports a vision of the place as dangerous and exotic, which some inexperienced travelers (or even experienced travelers) may already have in mind. It supports a heroic—as well as often gendered and racialized—approach

17. Kirby, *Equipped for Adventure.*

18. Wikipedia is a crowd-sourced reference, and thus can be edited by anyone at any time. The fact that the entry for this topic includes these ideas suggests that these are widely held and shared understandings in the English-speaking world. See "Adventure Film," *Wikipedia,* https://en.wikipedia.org/w/index.php?title=Adventure_film&oldid=962455519.

to missions which we know is a tendency for some United States travelers already.[19] To use the word "adventure" is certainly to foreground the experience of the traveler, which should strike us as problematic for anything that carries the title of "mission."

Images in our Imaginary

Perhaps as powerful (or more powerful) than the words we use are the images we select to associate with our STM. In 2005, *Christianity Today* (*CT*) magazine featured a prominent husband and wife pastoral team of a United States-based megachurch on the cover of their October issue. The story was on the plan for the church to send thousands of members on short-term mission teams around the world to facilitate the implementation of a multiyear development and evangelism plan, an ambitious work to support churches globally. Setting aside the plan itself, the first controversy to arise was this *CT* cover photo. The picture had the white couple standing in the middle of a large group of black children. The two white people in the photo popped out like beams of light from a sea of dark faces that stretched to every edge of the cover. In response, one letter to the editor of the magazine declared, "A picture alone is probably incapable of setting back by 50 years the American church's attitudes toward Africa, but October's cover made a valiant effort. Brightly lit, angelic white adults surrounded by childlike blackness—these are pictures that should be grimaced at and left on the darkroom floor, not splashed on magazine covers."[20] The photo was an extreme example of what I call the "smiley brown children photo" that shows up in many STM photo presentations.

What a photo like this does, as the author of the letter to *CT* suggests, is tap into a pre-existing social imaginary of Africa as The Dark Continent. Visually placing the white face in this "dark" space creates the sense that these are the hope for this benighted and needy world. Whether the smiley brown children are from Africa, Latin America, Asia, or the Middle East, the photo feeds a racialized imaginary that places the (usually white) STM

19. There is a virtual cottage industry writing about the White Savior Industrial Complex. One of the first to clearly identify this phenomenon was Teju Cole, who posted a series of tweets in 2012 in response to the family Kony 2012 campaign of the U.S. based group "Invisible Children." He followed that with an article in the Atlantic. See Cole, "The White-Savior Industrial Complex."

20. Grant, "Readers Write," 14.

team member in the position of helper and savior once again. It places those hosting the team in the position of the helpless receiver, rather than as a potential leader, teacher, or even a partner.

I have witnessed this dynamic for myself in dozens of presentations made in congregations or colleges where I have seen STM trips presented. In the congregation where I did my original research, I recall one team's presentation on their trip into Chicago, just thirty miles east of our suburb. Although this was not to an "exotic" locale, the presentation had many of these same photo traditions: photos of the "arrival," shots of small brown children crowding around to be photographed with the white teens from our church, "action" shots of the teens teaching the children. A few featured brown-skinned adults and older teens with their arms around our team members, but there were none that suggested the local Black adults served in leadership, teaching, or authority positions. The final photos featured just our team, in their matching shirts, ready to depart. All these photos depict real aspects of the STM work: friendship, service, camaraderie. Yet, particularly when decontextualized, they serve to reinforce the social imaginary of the white savior to the needy brown-skinned "native."[21]

Re-forming our Imaginary

Reforming the narratives that shape our short-term mission experiences requires attending to the words, phrases, and images we use to tell ourselves and others what it is that we did, or want to do. It doesn't mean there are perfect ways to talk about any of this. Every language is simultaneously a world of possibility, and an iron cage. We have many ways, in English for example, to say virtually anything we want to say. But we also have the structures of vocabulary, syntax, and grammar that make English English and not Tagalog, Amharic, or Xhosa. We cannot simply avoid speaking for fear that we cannot find the perfect words, but rather we should intentionally reflect on the words and images we choose in representing our work in

---

21. I saw these photos in a display hanging in the youth group room, with no text to explain the specific photos or other contextualizing information. These photos could be less implicated in some of these imaginaries if presented along with the names of everyone in the photo, hear something of the context in which it was taken, and perhaps receive greater understanding of the fully-orbed relationships involved. However, it is also common that such photos do not have names attached (particularly of the children), and may have little relational context.

order to avoid inadvertently forming the narrative around a social imaginary that inhibits or even mis-forms our lives and relationships.

Thinking more carefully about the social imaginary invoked by words like "partnership" or "adventure" allows us to consider what is implied by a word, and how we are shaping our own understanding of what we're seeking to do. Presenting images that depict the STM team members as learners, and the local community as complex, full of strong leaders and strategic resources in addition to suffering and poverty, begins to instill a new social imaginary out of which the STM narrative is drawn. Creative neologisms such as "copowerment" can create space in our social imaginaries for new understandings of the work and relationships in STM. Similarly, the languages in host countries may provide opportunities to enter into the social imaginaries of new communities. By spending time considering the effects of key words and images, we can have a conversation with a host community. We may learn if they understand the words as we do, what words might exist around these ideas in their own language, and how to reconcile the common vision that might emerge.[22]

As we seek to join God in his mission, we cannot be naïve to the patterns of this world that seek to conform us. We cannot ignore the kinds of images we choose or the words we use, because these are the building blocks of our expectations and narratives of these trips, by which we communicate the *meanings* of these trips to ourselves and others. In order to reform what these trips are, why and how we travel, and what they do in the Kingdom of God, we must not be conformed to the patterns of this world, but be transformed by the renewal of our minds.

Brian Howell

Brian Howell (MA, Fuller Seminary, MA/PhD, Washington University in St. Louis) is Professor of Anthropology at Wheaton College, in Wheaton, IL, where he has taught since 2001. He is the author of *Short Term Mission:*

---

22. The options in local languages are surely vast. One example would be the Filipino/ Tagalog word *pakikisama*. From the root "sama," meaning "together," it can be glossed "accompaniment" or more aptly "working alongside to accomplish _____." It includes notions of welcoming others, helping people feel comfortable, and seeing one's self as part of the whole. It is a complex term that has deep meaning for many people in the Philippines. If a visiting group framed their work as *pakikisama*, it could serve to reshape the imagination on the nature of the work and relationship. See Lynch and de Guzman, *Four Readings on Philippine Values.*

An Ethnography of Christian Travel Narrative and Experience, as well as a textbook on anthropology, *Introducing Cultural Anthropology: A Christian Perspective,* and books and articles on Christianity in the Philippines, anthropological research, and race in the United States. He lives in Wheaton with his wife, Marissa. They have three adult children of whom they are very proud.

Bibliography

Adeney, Miriam. "When the Elephant Dances, the Mouse May Die." In *When Helping Hurts: How to Alleviate Poverty Without Hurting the Poor . . . And Yourself,* edited by Steve Corbett and Brian Fikkert, 156–60. Chicago, IL: Moody Publishers, 2009.

Edward M. Bruner. "The Maasai and the Lion King: Authenticity, Nationalism, and Globalization in African Tourism." In *Tourist and Tourism,* edited by Sharon Gmelch, 208–36. Long Grove, IL: Waveland, 2004.

Certeau, Michel de. *The Practice of Everyday Life.* Berkeley: University of California Press, 1984.

Cohen, Erik. "Primitive and Remote: Hill Tribe Trekking in Thailand." *Annals of Tourism Research,* 16 (1989) 16.

Cole, Teju. "The White-Savior Industrial Complex." *The Atlantic. https://www.theatlantic.com/international/archive/2012/03/the-white-savior-industrial-complex/254843/.*

Grant, Richard. "Readers Write." *Christianity Today* 49, (2005).

Howell, Brian M. *Short-Term Mission: An Ethnography of Christian Travel Narrative and Experience.* Downers Grove, IL: IVP Academic, 2012.

Kirby, Scott. *Equipped for Adventure: A Practical Guide to Short-Term Mission Trips.* Birmingham, AL: New Hope, 2006.

Lederleitner, Mary. *Cross-Cultural Partnerships: Navigating the Complexities of Money and Mission.* Downers Grove, IL: InterVarsity, 2010.

Löfgren, Orvar. *On Holiday: A History of Vacationing.* Berkeley: University of California Press, 2010.

Lynch, F. and de Guzman, A. *Four Readings on Philippine Values.* Quezon City, Philippines: Ateneo de Manila University Press; 1974.

Offutt, Steve. "The Role of Short-Term Mission Teams in the New Centers of Global Christianity," *Scientific Study of Religion* 50, (2011) 796.

Robert J. Priest. "Short-Term Missions as a New Paradigm." In *Missions After Christendom: Emergent Themes in Contemporary Mission,* edited by Ogbu Kalu, Peter Vethanayagamony, and Edmund K. Chia, 84–100. Louisville, KY: Westminster John Knox, 2010.

Salazar, Noel B., and Graburn Nelson H H. *Tourism Imaginaries: Anthropological Approaches.* New York: Berghahn Books, 2016.

Stasch, Rupert. "Towards Symmetric Treatment of Imaginaries: Nudity and Payment in Tourism to Papua's 'Treehouse People.'" In *Tourism Imaginaries: Anthropological Approach,* edited by Noel B Salazar and Graburn H. H, Nelson, 31–57. New York: Berghahn, 2014.

Taylor, Charles. *Modern Social Imaginaries.* Durham: Duke University Press, 2007.

Discussion Questions

THE FOLLOWING QUESTIONS ARE meant to create "conversation" between this section's themes and your own perspectives and experiences. They are intended to be useful for both sides of the STM relationship: guests who travel to serve other communities, and the hosts who receive them. While these questions offer thought-provoking prompts for journaling, meditation, and prayer, they also serve as starting places for group discussion with others in your community who care about reimagining STM. We highly recommend both modes of engagement when that is possible.

1. How would you describe the difference between voyeuristic curiosity, and the sort of curiosity that leads to effective engagement in STM? How might the character quality of teachability help hosts and senders to work with one another as coequal members of the global church?

2. Corey Greaves suggests that SLAM trips were designed to resist unhelpful STM practices, and to model something closer to a new paradigm. What in your view are the important differences in the SLAM trip model, and how do they "disrupt bad practices?" Are there values and practices in this approach that might be applicable to other STM contexts you are familiar with?

3. Nathan Nelson suggests that trust is necessary for copowerment. What is the connection? In the STM settings he describes, how did

copowering practice yield better results for both the receiving and the sending communities? Is copowerment something that might make your community's STM practices more effective?

4. Craig Greenfield and other authors in this section make the case that short-term missions can be made more effective (and less destructive) only if hosts and senders "take the long view." What does that actually mean, and how does it run counter to the ways STM is usually done? If, as Bonita Broadnax and Brian Fikkert claim, "the likelihood of a church outreach team or missions group being able to build authentic relationships, locally or internationally, within the time limits of a typical short-term missions trip, service project, or outreach day is very low indeed," should we even be doing STM at all?

5. Several authors in this section, including Ben Beltran and Scott Bessenecker, suggest that a better way forward in short-term missions must include "reciprocal learning" and mutual transformation for those on both sides of a STM collaborative relationship. Do you think this goal is perhaps too idealistic? For those involved in hosting short-term teams, what would reciprocal transformation even look like for your community?

6. Think about the language your community uses to talk about short-term missions trips, and list some of the key words used to communicate about them to your community. What are the "imaginaries" behind the language, and how do they work to shape the ways people experience short-term missions trips?

SECTION FOUR

Creativity and Contextualization

MERE TWEAKING OF EXISTING short-term models will not be enough to hasten the sort of reform of STMs that is needed. It will take honest, critical thinking and courageous creativity to generate radical redesigns of the ways that we as the global church engage in STMs. The starting place in many cases will be the particularities of context. Not every trip or cross-cultural exchange should have to look the same. Rather, both those on the sending and receiving ends must look at the context in which God has placed them, and creatively reimagine how cross-cultural travel and relationships might be shaped in ways that better serve God's specific purposes in their unique contexts.

This approach of contextual innovation directly confronts elements of uncritical and uncreative thinking that make so many STM endeavors ineffective (and quite often, offensive). Americans in particular are prone to the hubris that allows them to make assertions like: "We used this model of mission among the poor in Guatemala, so this is obviously what you need to do in Thailand." This stance of assumed expertise keeps us from learning from our failures, because it never occurs to us that failure is an option. Even more damaging is the tendency among would-be helpers to avoid seeking the input and guidance of those they seek to serve—the locals who know their own context better than any outsider—and who, if asked, usually have a better sense of the challenges their communities face, and how they could be addressed if circumstances and resources allowed.

A more respectful, collaborative stance of coequality, on the other hand, brings together a diversity of perspectives and resources that tends to catalyze creativity. This invariably yields designs for transformative programs and processes that are more impactful because they are created to respond to the particularities of a place, and because they engage the capacities and resources of that place and its people. Thus the context-focused, essentially relational dynamic of copowerment creates a foundation for cross-cultural, collaborative engagements that yield long-term, sustainable results for all stakeholders.

14

Re-Symbolizing the White Van

AUSTIN ROBINSON

The White Van

WHEN I WAS FIFTEEN years old, I rode in the back of a white van with several other Christian youths into the San Quintin Valley in Baja California, Mexico. For many American Christian young people, a short-term mission trip like this is a rite of passage, an ultimate demonstration of faith. The people in the San Quintin Valley always recognized the large white van (which has become a ubiquitous symbol of short-term missions around the world) and knew exactly who we were and what we were doing. We spent the day playing with the children, and distributing toys, clothes, and food. Afterwards, everyone would line up for their tortilla-wrapped hot dog (and to our minds, this Mexican-American fusion was somehow meant to represent the unity of the global church). What always followed was a sermon or video expressing the gospel message, including an appeal to audience members to raise their hands and accept Jesus into their hearts. Each hand raised was a victory that we'd go home to share with our churches. Each year, I would look forward to my missionary journey. Until the day I moved to the San Quintin Valley.

It is now fifteen years after my first mission trip, and I've come to call the San Quintin Valley my home for almost a decade. I am the cofounder and Executive Director of Eternal Anchor, a ministry serving children and adults with disabilities in Mexico. As the region continues to attract countless short-term mission volunteers in their rented white vans, I've found myself processing short-term trips both as an insider and an outsider. While a short-term trip first led me to Mexico, once I moved here it didn't take long to deconstruct my misconceptions about the true value of short-term mission work.

Right away, my perspective changed as I became more in tune with how local churches, organizations, and individuals viewed STMs. I learned that what I considered to be spontaneity in participating in a last-minute trip was, in fact, recklessness—not having taken the time to communicate with the host organization, reflect on the purpose of the trip, or prepare my soul. I learned that the projects that made me feel accomplished—the cleaning, weeding, and painting—were usually work designed to keep teams occupied, and often created more work for the host organization than help. I learned that my heroic sacrifice to spend time with orphans (many with families and who were often incorrectly labeled "orphan"), was actually fueling severe attachment disorders that many suffered from. I learned how handouts of food, clothes, and toys create unhealthy dependencies, damage local economies, and undercut local church efforts. I learned that facilitating unsupervised play between children and foreign strangers desensitizes children to the dangers of abuse and abduction. I learned that taking selfies with poor children, and pictures that highlight poverty, perpetuates savior complexes while inciting feelings of shame and inferiority in the local community. I learned that most of the people that I was proud to convert were already Christians and were mostly there for the free handouts. And I learned that our attempt to combine traditional Mexican tortillas and American hot dogs actually tastes awful. And I came to understand that, to many in the San Quintin Valley, the white van was a symbol of these unhelpful, sometime-damaging practices

There is a desperate need to redeem short-term missions. The practice of short-term trips—typically a week or two spent volunteering in a foreign, high-poverty context—has become broken and often toxic—*yet still holds great potential for advancing social justice causes and manifesting God's perfect love to people who are oppressed and marginalized around the globe.* With humility, I offer here my own experience as a former participant of

STMs and current host, to share stories of individuals (including myself) who have caused harm during STMs and, in contrast, those who have formed healthy, joyful partnerships through STMs. As with all positive change, the key is leaning into the core Christian values of humility, trust, and love to foster a new era of collaboration and mutuality in STMs.

Ditching the Agenda

One aspect of STMs that stands in the way of healthy global partnerships is the dangerous conquest mentality that many groups bring with them. They have quotas they feel they must meet to justify their trip. Efforts are dedicated to building a certain number of homes, converting a certain number of people, and giving a quota of toys or food bags. There is an entitlement to operate unsupervised and impose charity campaigns in an unknown community with no knowledge of the religious, social, cultural, or economic context. I've even seen teams that think it's okay to coordinate medical campaigns with unskilled, uneducated volunteers, and facilitate construction projects without an experienced contractor supervising. The results are often disastrous, but the prevailing mentality is: "It's good enough for Mexico."

A better approach is to allow trusted host organizations to delegate the funds and efforts in the way they see fit. As Nathan Nelson points out, trusting and deferring to the local leaders opens the doors for copowerment, where communities and visitors can work alongside one another, learn from each other, and collaborate for positive change.[1] Practically, sending the organization a list of team members's skill sets and language abilities allows the hosts to decide how best to utilize talents and professional abilities to benefit their projects and programs. If visiting teams are concerned about how their talents and knowledge are utilized, they should find an organization that best aligns with their professional experience, credentials, and passion.

John: A Story about Harmful Agendas

As a case in point, let me tell you about an experience that occurred about a year after I moved to Mexico. John, an American church member, had brought down multiple groups to volunteer at different non-profit

1. See Nathan Nelson's observations in chapter 10 of this volume, 121–131.

organizations in the San Quintin Valley. Before coming, he polled his team and asked where they wanted to plug in for the week. He then reached out to the organization and told them when his team would like to come and what they would like to do. Some teams wanted to raise money for house construction, some wished to volunteer at women's shelters, and others preferred to do outreach campaigns that consisted of handouts, medical consults, or evangelism.

A few years back, John reached out to Dana, a good friend of mine who was the director of her organization's community outreach department. John had a long history with this particular organization. Dana and her predecessors had facilitated hundreds of John's outreach campaigns over the years. However, this time Dana asked if John would be willing to try something different. She had come to learn that handouts, medical appointments, and evangelism campaigns were not the most effective way to facilitate sustainable community development, and in some cases these efforts were actually hurting grassroots efforts. After spending time in the community, talking to locals, and assessing the needs from the perspective of community members, she discovered that adult literacy rates were abysmal. She asked John if he would partner with her staff to host adult literacy classes by helping them with childcare for the students' children. This would entail coordinating arts and crafts, coming up with group games, and assisting with the Bible teaching. This partnership would free up more of her staff to focus on tutoring students, improving the quality and impact of their program.

John did not want to disappoint his team, who loved handing out care packages and praying over new converts. So he went over Dana's head and contacted her organization's American board of directors to give an ultimatum: either they continue to facilitate his agenda, or he would take his team and money elsewhere. John understood that most non-profit organizations, especially those operating internationally, depend on the donations of visiting teams. He knew that he controlled the flow of potential new donors and could easily redirect the hundreds of future volunteers he coordinated to a different organization. The American board of directors—those responsible for funding operations—also knew this, and so allowed John to impose his team's to-do list on local leadership to protect precious donations.

Dana was understandably frustrated and discouraged. John failed to understand how his actions disempowered her and her team. He allowed his agenda to take precedence over her ideas and initiatives, undermining her authority and creativity. If John would have been willing to ditch his agenda and accept the tasks that were requested of him and his team, he could have helped foster a new, better approach to short-term missions that respects and empowers local leaders. If he would have humbled himself, he and his team could have learned important transformational lessons, and been edified by the example of the host organization in its passionate devotion to the good of the community. Sadly, even several years later, John continues to bring teams and impose his agenda. The few organizations that assert their preferences or guidelines for foreign visitors are sidestepped, and his teams and resources are directed only to organizations that will facilitate his teams's wishes. In order to improve STMs, we need to recognize this common, unhealthy power dynamic between host and visiting team, and work to dismantle it by ensuring that STM leaders are prepared for the potential of letting go of their own agendas and embracing humility in coequal partnerships with other members of the global church.

Making Friends

To continue our reformation of STMs, we must address what should be at the center of any short-term trip: relationships. While relationships are the crux of STMs, teams often create a visible social divide between themselves and the community they are partnering with when they pile out of their vehicles with their matching team t-shirts and bandanas. Similarly, the relational divide is deepened if teams do not take the time to learn some of the language, and instead assume that locals will understand their shouts and gestures. And when they "take" (literally) their hundreds of photos whose main purpose it is to chronicle their service successes, they demean and relegate communities to the role of needy recipient, stripping away control and dignity from them. Though typically unintentional, the assumption appears to be that God is not already active in these communities through efforts of local leaders and organizations.

In contrast, imagine if teams were to arrive with a posture of humility and openness. Imagine how meaningful it would be for a community in Mexico if the visiting team came with an attitude of teachability, spending time learning as much of the native language as they could, demonstrating an intentionality to build meaningful relationships with their hosts. Imagine if teams were to let go of their own plans and answers, and instead showed up in humility with the expectation to learn and observe how God is already at work in foreign communities. Imagine what it would mean to the community if teams listened to the expertise of local leaders and were inspired by what was already being accomplished in the community. Imagine the message it would send to the churches back home, if the pictures from that trip celebrated the dignity and strength of the host community, honored the hard work of locals, and highlighted new emerging friendships between volunteers and hosts. When true relationships are the center of STMs, many of the pitfalls of STMs are avoided—and dignity, mutuality, and progress are fostered instead.

Nicki: A Story about Forming Friendships

When I first moved to Mexico, my interactions with short-term mission teams were largely those of a spectator. They would come, do their thing, and leave. My interactions were limited, partially because I had limited social energy, and partially because their agendas rarely overlapped with the work I was doing with disabled children. This changed when I became the director of a local organization and began coordinating visiting teams wanting to partner with us. Early on, I felt conflicted. I knew that visiting teams brought vital donations, and as director of a brand-new organization I couldn't overlook this necessary source of operations income. However, I wondered if welcoming visiting teams would somehow compromise what we were doing. Would allowing strangers to partner with us ultimately help or harm us? I wondered if short-term mission trips could be something more than what I had learned to expect. That's when I met Nicki.

Nicki was one of the very first people to lead a short-term mission team to partner with my organization. Almost immediately, I knew Nicki was different from other STM team leaders. Unlike other groups I've worked with, her team's primary focus has always been building relationships with our staff and clients. While most team leaders carry themselves with an air of superiority, Nicki is the humblest person I've ever met. After multiple trips, she has become a friend to many of the teachers and education coordinators at our special education school. Not only does she make time during the week to visit with the staff members and encourage them, but she is intentional about keeping in touch throughout the year. She regularly advocates for her church to send multiple teams to visit us in order to strengthen the bonds between her church family and our community of staff and students. Prior to visiting, team members who sign up are asked to participate in language training (in person or online) to ensure that they have a basic grasp of Spanish. She also sends the school staff a list of the volunteers, their talents and professional experience, and asks if they can raise money for a specific project or need. The school director is always grateful for this because other teams ask to do needless painting projects and bring unnecessary donations in bulk. Before coming, Nicki makes sure her team has multiple meetings to prepare their hearts and minds to not only partner in the work my organization is doing, but to be inspired by it and to respond to it in their own community.

When they arrive, Nicki makes sure that her team prioritizes the detailed orientation that my organization offers so that they have a clear understanding of our expectations. They spend the week helping as teacher assistants, tutors, and janitors. Each afternoon, she invites different staff members from our school to dinner, to get to know them better and to help her team learn more about the culture and people of the region. At the end of the week, her team hosts a feast to share with our organization's staff and their families. Everyone plays games, shares stories around a bonfire, and swaps contact information with their new friends. At the end, she shares words of encouragement to the staff and invites her team members to do the same.

Throughout the year, Nicki asks us for updates and shares prayer requests and stories of success with her church. The church, in turn, shares their prayer needs and celebrations with us. Friends stay in touch via email and social media. When visiting teams return, it feels like a family reunion. *This is the global church in action.* Nicki's intentionality in prioritizing relationships and friendships over accomplishing a predetermined agenda is what has always set her apart. Her posture of love and humility make it easy to work with her and her team. Her team makes room for mutuality, encouraging both visitors and hosts to learn from one another and celebrate one another. After five years of partnership, everyone in my organization looks forward to hosting teams from her church, even when she's unable to come. She has laid a foundation of a healthy friendship that has blossomed and blessed both my organization and her church.

Stop Calling it a "Short-Term Mission Trip"

CRAIG GREENFIELD

IMAGINE IF I WERE to write this letter to my local dentist:

> *"Dear Sir, I'd like to come and be a dentist for two weeks.*
> *I've been meeting once a month with a small group of oth-*
> *ers who also want to be short-term dentists, and we have*
> *our t-shirts printed and we're ready to come.*
> *P.S. Can you drive us around, translate for us, and help us*
> *take cool photos for our Facebook pages?"*

I'd like to be a fly on the wall when the dentist receives that letter.

Perhaps it's time we recognize that most of what we call "short-term missions trips" are not "missions" at all. If our mission is to go and make disciples of the nations, how can we make a single disciple if we can't even speak their language?[2] With a tract? How can we teach someone to follow Jesus in five days? With a handy flow-chart? How do we transform a situation of poverty or trafficking? With a Christmas shoebox? Nope. None of the above. Jesus spent thirty *years* immersed in one culture before launching his ministry. And he was the Son of God! When he sent out his own disciples two by two, they went to places where they spoke the language and understood the culture already. They went as cultural insiders, not cultural outsiders. And they went empty-handed.[3] So, let's reexamine the label, "short-term missions" and replace it with something that will better reflect what is really going on.

We don't have short-term social workers, or short-term bioscientists. We don't have short-term gastroenterologists or short-term politicians. So why do we have short-term missionaries in ever-increasing numbers? Here's the problem: we've created in our minds a false continuum. At one end of the continuum is "short-term missions" and at the other end is something we call

2. Matt 28:19 (NIV).
3. Luke 9:3 (NIV).

"long-term missions." We think of them as pretty much the same thing, but with differing lengths of service. But they're not the same. And by naming them both "mission" we may be missing the point.

It might help at this point to situate "long-term missions" properly. Let's agree that there is no such thing as a part-time Christian. There is no such thing as a follower of Jesus who is not in full-time service to God. If you are a full-time banker, and a part-time Christian—you might be deluded. Which begs the question, what do we mean when we say we are going into "full-time Christian ministry?" What were we doing up to this point?

As followers of Jesus, we are all called to a *vocation*. That's the term we need to embrace. It will put everything else in its proper place. Our vocation, whether in butchering, baking or candlestick-making—is the primary means we have been given to serve God. Some of us will have a vocation as an architect or a writer, as a parent or a nurse. And some of us will have a vocation in cross-cultural service among the poor. Humanitarian work, Bible translation, social entrepreneurship—these have all been lumped into a catch-all category called "long-term missions"—but they are just different variations on *every* Christian's call to pursue a vocation that serves God, and God's upside-down kingdom. When we see that each of us has a unique and important vocation, we'll no longer single out some as more spiritual than others. We'll support and pray for all equally. And we'll develop a theology of work that works.

Now that we understand how the "long-term missions" has been unhelpfully differentiated from anyone else's vocation, we can better understand why "short-term missions" is such a misleading term. Again, these short-term missions trips are generally not "mission." They are not part of a vocation to serve cross-culturally among the poor because a vocation does not take place in two weeks or two years.

So, what is it we are really trying to say with the descriptor "short-term missions?" In many cases, a primary motivation for these trips is learning and personal transformation. When that is the case, consider three more honest and accurate alternatives names for such "short-term mission" trips:

Vision (or Exposure) Trips

A focused intentional time where we ask God to open our hearts to the plight of the poor. What the eye has not seen the heart cannot grieve over. So, it's natural that when people find themselves face to face with poverty for the first time, something significant happens. The rest of our lives are irrevocably shaped by what we have witnessed. We gain vision.

Learning Exchanges

A time when our theology and understanding of the world is rocked to the core and deconstructed. When we travel as learners, eager to have our minds expanded and preconceptions challenged, we will not be disappointed. This category includes those who travel as part of their vocation—as a builder, surgeon or dentist for example—but are open to learning from God while they are passing on expertise to others in another country.

Discernment Retreats

A time when we seek vocational discernment at the margins. To pursue a vocation in any field without having a perspective that takes into account the world's poor (among whom God's heart and good news is centered) is folly. How can we be a banker for God, if we don't know how the financial services industry affects the poor? How can we be an architect or planner for God, if we don't know how the design of cities affects the homeless? How can we be a teacher, if we don't bring the reality of the world's poorest to our students? These trips have the potential to reshape our vocation (and we might for example choose to serve overseas from time to time), or even to spark the discovery of new vocations.

In short, there is no such thing as a two-week vocation. And there is no such thing as "short-term missions." Let's get our labels right, and hopefully our practices and understanding will follow.

Craig Greenfield

Craig Greenfield is the founder of Alongsiders International, a grassroots discipleship movement of eight thousand children and youth across Asia and Africa. He is the author of *Subversive Jesus* and the upcoming book, *Outsider Calling*. Visit his blog at www. craiggreenfield.com

Asking Questions

A third component that is essential to recreate STMs is knowing what questions to ask. While some short-term mission teams bulldoze local leaders with imposed agendas, other teams blindly fund organizations that have no real positive impact in their community. To prevent this, some research and investigation is required to ensure that prospective partner organizations are operating with integrity and excellence. Some important questions to ask before forming a long-term relational and financial partnership include:

1. How are local leaders empowered and supported to make decisions and take risks without foreign interference?

2. How does the organization demonstrate financial transparency and integrity?

3. How are programs and projects evaluated?

4. What is the reputation of the organization in the community?

5. How does the organizational structure facilitate accountability and empowerment?

These questions help keep organizations accountable and help foreign teams feel more confident in their choice to partner with the organization. Ideally, questions would be asked in person on a preliminary vision trip. This would serve as an opportunity to both build a relationship with the host organization's leadership and staff, as well as give the visitors the chance to experience first-hand the effectiveness and impact the organization is having in the community.

David: A Story about Harmful Ignorance

One of the most illuminating examples of the dangers of not asking questions involves a pastor from Canada and a children's home just a few hours from my home. David's church has a robust missions budget that allows them to partner with many different international organizations. Recently, David received an email with a plea for help from a special needs children's home in Mexico. David saw this as a great opportunity to diversify his church's mission work. They were already funding organizations in Uganda, Syria, Ukraine, and Indonesia. In his mind, a Latin American partnership would round out his church's missional involvement.

After a few months of dialogue, David led a small exploratory team to visit the children's home. When he arrived, he was greeted by a bilingual couple in charge of the home. The building was freshly painted, but it was obvious there were serious maintenance needs. Windows were cracked, shutters falling off the wall, and a leaky pipe in the front yard left everyone holding their breath. When they entered the building, they saw thirty children with profound special needs. Most were in wheelchairs that lined the walls of the main room or were laying in their soiled beds. They were dirty, many were crying, and there were flies swarming their faces. There were only three staff members and it was obvious they had their hands full with cooking, cleaning, and caretaking. The directors gave them a brief tour of the home and shared the challenges of running the home with minimal funding. They shared their passion for caring for children who have been abandoned by their families and stigmatized by society.

David and his team spent a few days helping with the cleaning and maintenance work. They left with tears in their eyes and resolved to partner with the organization to provide higher quality care for the children. Before leaving, they left a sizable check and promised that more money and more teams were on the way.

David didn't ask questions and failed to learn some scary truths about his church's new partner organization. The director of the organization is actually an American man who has a reputation of siphoning money from the children's home to feed a drug addiction. The local directors are known to manipulate visiting teams by keeping the installations in poor conditions and the children unbathed and unhappy as a fundraising strategy. In spite of sufficient funding, they refuse to hire more staff so the directors can pay themselves robust salaries. The children's home has been condemned by Mexican Child Protective Services and international disability rights organizations for the use of cages, and their practice of allowing any family to abandon their child at the facility without going through government agencies. David and his church are now providing substantial funding to an organization that is exploiting and abusing children.

In this case, the directors of this children's home view STMs as a source of blind funding. And because of examples of irresponsible funding like this, the government and other local organizations that are operating with integrity associate STMs with ignorance, and with a system that undermines the integrity of the work they are trying to accomplish. These perceptions demonstrate the serious need for short-term mission leaders to ask the right questions and become competent allies of the work being done in foreign communities.

Giving Generously

STMs have the ability to contribute to one of the most challenging and important tasks of any non-profit organization. Hosting trips is a great opportunity to expand networks and create sustainable donor bases. However, this only works when team members make financial commitments beyond their one-week visit. Too often, people are willing to raise thousands of dollars for travel expenses, but are unwilling to send a monthly donation for the host organization's operations. To put it bluntly, these organizations would often prefer to not host visitors who do not want to become long-term financial partners. They would rather utilize their time, energy, and resources to build relationships with people who believe in the mission of the organization, understand the importance of sustainable funding, and are willing to make a long-term financial commitment.

Marsha: A Story about Financial Commitment

Marsha was one of the first people to visit our school after we opened a few years ago. I met her and her team and introduced them to a few local volunteers and the dozens of community members benefiting from our services. Over the last five years, Marsha has returned multiple times with the same team to visit the school. They've watched the program grow and have witnessed the incredible impact it has had on our community. They've experienced firsthand how facilitating access to special education can transform a community, giving hope to families who are typically forced to leave their children with special needs locked up while they work. They can vouch for the financial integrity of my organization and our standards of excellence. Yet, after five years of visiting, Marsha has never given a penny to the school. She and her team raise enough money for their flights, van rentals, meals, hotels, and souvenirs, but they never bring project money and not a single team member has signed up to donate monthly.

It is discouraging because after five years of coordinating visits, it feels like Marsha and her team don't really appreciate or value our work. It feels like none of them believe in our mission or vision. It feels like they don't trust us or care about us beyond the one-week stay. When Marsha comes, I secretly dread the visit, knowing that I have to take time out of my busy schedule to entertain guests who have no interest in truly partnering with my organization. I don't dare tell Marsha this, because despite her historical lack of giving, she still represents a potential funding source that I can't totally disregard. When I see her team arrive, I sigh and put on a fake smile. I know deep down that the time I spend with her and her team will likely be unproductive. If after five years they haven't given, do they really care about what we do? Yet, I welcome them with the hope that one day they may have a change of heart and become true partners in the work we do, sacrificing not just their time but their money to help us accomplish our mission.

Leveraging Privilege

The apex of most short-term mission trips is the reflection meeting at the end of the week. Sitting around a bonfire, teams end their visit with teary eyes as they sing songs, reminisce about their efforts and accomplishments, and share epiphanies of poverty and privilege. While it is vital to recognize privilege, this cannot be the purpose of short-term mission trips. If the only takeaway from a trip is a renewed appreciation for one's social, political, and economic state, then pity becomes the overarching theme of the experience. Instead, the recognition of privilege should be a catalyst to seek out ways to leverage it in order to support and complement local and international social justice efforts.

Karly: A Story about Action

It was a sacrifice for Karly to go on her first short-term mission trip. Fresh out of graduate school, she had massive student debt and the burden of finding a new job. However, she was invited by a friend to utilize her skills as a speech therapist and volunteer at my organization. When she arrived at our school, she was amazed. She instantly fell in love with the staff, the clients, and the community. She humbly worked alongside our teachers and social workers, offering training and curriculum advice. She provided free consults to families and left recommendations with the program directors. Karly didn't leave with a sense of accomplishment, but instead with a deep sense of urgency.

She saw the need for more sustainable funding for my growing organization, so she signed up to donate monthly and encouraged her friends and family to do the same. She saw the need for more professionals to visit and provide training and consults, so she sent out an email to all of her colleagues and professional contacts inviting them to join her on her next trip. Most importantly, she saw the need to replicate the beautiful work being done in Mexico in her own community and in her own church. How could it be that this organization was doing so much with so little when her own church family was doing nothing to alleviate the suffering caused by disability in their community? She was empowered and inspired to leverage her privilege and the privilege of her church to make a difference in her town. She worked with her pastor and Sunday school teachers to create a more inclusive religious education program. She invited a local disability parent support group to host meetings at their church, providing free snacks and refreshments. She even began writing letters to her political representatives to advocate for more accessible public transportation options so people with disabilities could experience a higher level of participation in community activities and events. Karly's short-term mission trip was not the apex of her mission experience; it was the beginning of a life-long commitment and passion to manifest love and inclusion for people with disabilities in Mexico and in her hometown.

The difference between Karly and other short-term mission volunteers was her ability to see the trip as a small piece of a larger calling. She knew that sacrificing her time and money to partner with my organization meant so much more than a week-long trip to feel good about helping others. She saw the trip as an opportunity to learn how disability services can be offered in high-poverty contexts. She was excited to meet people who could fuel her passion to support and partner with families impacted by disability. She accepted her responsibility to not only help those struggling across international boundaries, but to also work alongside grassroots organizations in her own community. Karly learned how to recognize her privileged position as a well-off, educated American and leverage her resources and experiences to be a more credible, effective ally to people with special needs.

The Renewed STM

Every host organization has a secret list of short-term mission groups they love having back, and groups that they receive with reluctance. Teams that host organizations dread are characterized by pride, insensitivity, inconsistency, and carelessness. They mistakenly believe that STMs bring the gospel to foreign communities, instead of being inspired by the community leaders that are already manifesting the gospel in a powerful way. They are more concerned with meeting quotas and feeling accomplished than they are learning, making friends, and becoming competent, long-term allies. It is easier to be part of an ignorant team. It requires less planning, feeds egos and savior complexes, and doesn't demand a long-term financial or relational commitment. Sadly, that is why many STMs, arriving in their large white vans with their matching t-shirts, have become a negative symbol to those living in the host communities.

Yet, there is hope for change. Leaders like Nicki and Karly have demonstrated how traditional short-term mission trip practices can be changed by embracing humility, trust, and love. They reject the narrative that portrays visiting teams as noble saviors, while humbly seeking opportunities to learn from and be inspired by host communities. They trust that God is already active in these communities through the efforts of local leaders and organizations, and that their role is to support and encourage the efforts that precede and continue long after their visit. They truly love their foreign friends and believe in the work they are accomplishing. They are always careful to not demean, diminish, or damage local efforts.

When churches and short-term mission agencies start taking the time to prepare their teams, communicate with partner organizations, ask the right questions, defer to local leaders, and make long-term commitments, their presence will act as a spark for copowerment and collective action that will strengthen the global church. Instead of bringing superiority and handouts, white vans will deliver friendship and encouragement. When desire for authentic relationships replaces a savior mentality—and when self-oriented agendas and assumptions of expertise give way to trust and respect for local leaders and their initiatives—the white van might become a symbol of hope, love, and reciprocity, rather than one of disruptive, insensitive charity. Only then will short-term mission teams reflect the relational, loving essence of the gospel and have a powerful, positive impact on the communities they seek to serve.

Austin Robinson

Austin Robinson is the cofounder and Executive Director of Eternal Anchor, an NGO dedicated to alleviating the suffering caused by disability in rural Mexico, and combating the systems and stigmas that prevent people with disabilities from being celebrated and included as valued members of the community.

15

Path from Poverty
The Shared Work of Authentic Relationship

Agnes Kioko *and* Boni Piper

Path From Poverty

(www.pathfrompoverty.org) is a Seattle-based 501(c)(3) nonprofit organization that reaches across cultures to transform lives and communities by partnering with women's groups to empower and equip women to break the cycle of poverty and live into their God-given potential. In addition to the community development aspects of their work, PFP has found that catalyzing cross-cultural friendships has become a primary purpose and motivation for short-term trips. What follows is an account of that ongoing journey, told by two women who have become good friends through their involvement with PFP: Agnes Kioko and Boni Piper. Here they share their experiences in leading women to fully embrace an egalitarian and transforming copowerment model for sisters in Christ that spans the globe and bridges many differences.

Agnes: I joined a Path From Poverty (PFP) group in 2004. As I eagerly participated in all that was offered in PFP groups, I developed leadership skills and was elected group leader in my group of thirty women. In 2006, I became a Regional Program Manager, elected by all the groups in my region. This involved being on the leadership team that directs the Kenyan work. I now have fourteen groups in my region and am training another woman to help with these groups. In 2015, I was elected as the Regional Program Director of all PFP groups in Kenya. That means I am currently the head of the leadership team and all the work in Kenya.

Boni: In 2014, I went to Kenya on a Path From Poverty short-term mission trip. I was greatly impressed by the work and the model and all that was being accomplished, and felt a strong call from God to devote my life to this mission. Since then, I have been on the board of directors of PFP and have been chair of the board since 2015.

In our work together, Agnes and I have become good friends. Of course, when we bring the teams of American women to Kenya, we have a lot to talk about and collaborate on. But our friendship is so much more than that. We also talk personally about our lives. We often stay up late when others have gone to bed just so we can talk. We get each other's stories, and make each other laugh so hard! I am grateful that we can connect over social media. Still, we miss each other a lot when I'm not in Kenya.

Our friendship would not have been possible though if the practices of Path From Poverty didn't emphasize coequality between the Kenyan women and the American women on the visiting teams. She would never have tried to be real friends without my invitation to do that and vice versa. There are a lot of cross-cultural factors that work against forming real relationships.

Agnes: In the early days of team visits, I remember many things that originally were not "allowed"—dynamics that kept the two groups apart and kept both sides from having an authentic relationship. When it came to foreign visitors, Kenyans were taught we were not to communicate directly with anyone on the team, ever. There was to be no hugging, shaking hands, eating together or even sitting at the same table! Of course, we never slept in the same guest house, or had conversations that revealed much about our personal histories. And while the Americans were given chicken to eat, it was too costly for Kenyans to enjoy. We all assumed that all this is what Americans wanted—that they did not want to be close to us. That we were dirty.

Eventually, these things were revealed to the American women, who apparently knew nothing about these unspoken rules. When we took the risk to speak up about these misunderstandings, it was a fearful time for us Kenyans. We were so afraid of what might happen! We didn't like how we felt being around the Americans, but at least we had a working partnership with a good nonprofit. What would happen if we spoke up and as a result had that taken away? Oh, it was such a risk!

It turned out to be a risk worth taking though. Together we shared openly with our American colleagues about our fears and concerns. We cried together over our misunderstandings, and the limitations that had been forced on us by others who thought they knew better. We confessed our sins against each other, and offered forgiveness that was so needed.

Boni: In light of that communication breakthrough, after much prayer and discussion changes began to happen. Mission teams in the United States started spending many hours in training before leaving for Kenya. We learned the many ways Kenyan culture is quite different from American culture. We take so many things for granted and often believe that the way we see things is the way things are. What a presumption! I remember a year we worked at a house that was fairly nice. A team member said, "I could live here! They are not poor!" The two-room home, with its mud walls and dirt floor, was unlike any I had ever seen in the United States, but it was well cared for and comfortable for those who lived there. However, the woman in this home spent six hours a day walking to retrieve dirty water. The family had no electricity or plumbing. What seemed like a cute little house still held a level of poverty that most westerners knew little about.

The United States mission teams began to understand that the Kenyan women look to them to set parameters in terms of closeness and communication. American teams now understand that if they arrive with warm greetings and hugs, ready to dance and sing, the Kenyans will respond likewise. If we honestly tell our life stories, we will hear theirs as well. If we hold back our warmth and ourselves, the Kenyans will do the same. We, the visitors, will most likely determine if the trip will yield a relationally superficial experience, or a deep knowing of each other. The Kenyans will take their cue from us, as we learned from the Kenyan leaders.

Path From Poverty's work in Kenya has always been plagued by the ugly legacy of colonialism. While this is changing, in the early days of our work Kenyans were made to feel inferior, thinking whites wanted to feel superior. It takes real effort not to fall into that trap of that legacy of brokenness. But we have learned from experience that our colleagues in Kenya are just as capable as we are—and in fact are *more* capable when it comes to guiding the work of our common mission. We have a true partnership, meaning that we are equal in the governance of our common work, and equal in the dynamics of our relationships. We listen carefully to each other and value each other's opinions. Good relationships certainly take a lot of intentionality, though. We believe the kinds of relationships that Path From Poverty makes possible between the two cultures is unusual in cross-cultural missions.

It is worth noting that Path From Poverty was formed twenty years ago when two women, one from Kenya and one from the United States, met while working side by side on a mission project in a third country. They realized they both had a heart for women living in poverty and wanted to respond. Together they developed an egalitarian, self-sustaining model that proved effective in helping women transform their lives. Today that model aims to improve women's lives through listening to what *they* determine they need, and supporting *their* plan to meet it, rather than implementing what westerners think they need. This powerful distinction permeates all of PFP's work.

Agnes: Because they chose to trust us to know our needs and the best ways to meet them, PFP began to partner with us to reach our goals. That's the reason that, when the American PFP teams are with us, we make sure to dedicate time to helping them understand our lives, and listening to them share about their own.

For example, we help them to understand that our women and our daughters walk miles each day for water that is not clean, and we face violence, including rape and abduction, along the way. It takes many hours each day to find water, and when we find it it usually is contaminated by cholera, typhoid, and other deadly diseases. Boiling this water may not take away all diseases, and as a result our family members are often sick. Nearly every woman I know has family members who have died of waterborne diseases.

Since we live quite far apart on homesteads that have been inherited, building costly wells would not fulfill the need, as we would still have to walk many miles to the wells and carry the water home. Besides, the water just beneath the surface is salty, so the wells would have to be very deep and cost thousands of dollars. As Kenyan women discussed this problem, we decided that the best option for us would be to buy water tanks to catch the rain at our homes during the two main rainy seasons. This was the solution that we presented to Path From Poverty's representatives in the United States.

As part of the strategy we developed together, several groups of twenty to thirty women were formed in Kenya. We began learning things like effective leadership, record keeping, and improved hygiene at home. We also studied scripture and prayed together. We shared income-generating projects and began to work collectively. One topic that we discussed together was: What is our greatest need and how do we meet it? Eventually most decided that their greatest need was clean water and after that, solar power. These needs we shared with our American partners.

As our groups collectively saved money for water tanks—and later, solar panels—PFP US raised money for additional water tanks and solar panels. We knew that if we saved enough for one tank, another would be provided by PFP US. Knowing they would gift additional water tanks and panels in this way was a great incentive for the women who struggled so much to earn extra money to contribute to group savings. We continued to work this way until all the women in our groups received a water tank. This gifting model is the way the partnership has continued to operate now for twenty years.

Boni: As Agnes explained, we do our part of the collaborative work by raising funds to purchase some of the additional equipment. And to foster the relational context for our shared work, groups of us will visit Kenya to see the results of our collaborations and to spend time with our Kenyan sisters.

While we do actual physical work when we are there—usually helping to build the concrete bases for new water tanks—we understand that the real value comes from just being present. We are there to love, to bear witness to the stories we hear, to affirm and empower those we meet. We are also there as learners, knowing that empowerment goes both ways. We expect that westerners who go will be changed forever when they encounter women who are joyful and loving—even those who experience poverty and other adverse circumstances. It is so much more about *being* than *doing*; it is mainly about opening our hearts to one another. It is easy to dig a hole. It is much harder to keep an open heart and stay attentive to God's leading. That is part of what PFP training is about: learning to listen to God's Spirit. Becoming aware of what is happening around us. Stepping into the openings for loving action that we sense are ours. The foundation of PFP rests on the belief that we are truly children of one God, and therefore we are sisters. We believe that Jesus loves us equally and longs for us to love each other deeply.

Every year that I go to Kenya I learn so much, yet I return thinking I understand less of the culture than ever. Having traveled and lived in other cultures in my life, I am aware there are differences in traditions. Going back to Kenya year after year has made me aware of how superficially westerners truly understand the different cultures they work in. We learn a little and call it good! Most of us only touch the surface of our differences and claim to know enough. But in returning year after year, growing the Kenyan and American relationship, we learn a lot more about each other. This has helped me to know how much I don't understand and to learn to ask for help.

One of the cultural differences I became aware of involved the differences in the Kenyan concept of ownership. On one of my early work team trips, I was sent to gather up the tools we brought in order to take them home with us. We planned to bring them back to use again next year when we returned. Thankfully, Agnes quietly told me that we were appearing to be very greedy with our goods. Surely we could afford to leave the tools for the Kenyans to use in our absence. I was doing what I had been told to do and what I thought was expected. Looking back, I see how it must have looked to take the tools, only to keep them in storage, rather than allow them to be used throughout the year. In American culture, taking home what you bring is a normal thing to do, but in a collective culture it didn't seem right. And it went against what we were teaching. We encouraged the groups to share their information, their ideas for making money. They always share their goods, their food, their water. Americans like to share knowledge, but it is not our practice to share goods; we even call them *possessions*. Kenyans have taught us to be more aware of our reluctance to share what we value, our things, and have prompted us to remember this tendency, even when making board decisions in the Unites States.

Another area in my life where I have learned to overcome cultural presumptions has to do with leadership. I have so many examples of having to hold myself back from taking over a group project, only to realize that I never really had a sense of what was going on to begin with. A few years ago, I was in Kenya with a United States team building cement bases for the water tanks the women had earned. This is our usual work, using supplies paid for by PFP US, and it helps the poorer women who receive water tanks because base construction is costly. Our work team was waiting for the Kenyan women to decide which three or four westerners were going to which house to build a base. From an American point of view, it was an easy decision because it seemed it really didn't matter who went where.

We had been waiting in the hot sun for direction for over thirty minutes when my American team members began to beg me to just make the decision! I wouldn't do it though, and I reminded them that this was the very thing we had talked about in our training. We did not know why it was taking the Kenyan women so much time to make this decision. But if I had a Kenyan mind, I would probably understand better. The question for us as Americans was, "What does God have for us in this moment, and what is God showing me about myself right now?" Oh, but it would have been so much easier to simply make the decision! But for me to assume the role of decision maker in that situation would have been wrong. It takes years to help women become empowered to change their lives, but only a few times of us overriding or rejecting that empowerment for them to lose what they had worked to gain.

Agnes: For the most part, the visiting teams really are a benefit to the women in Kenya. To be honest though, there are also some difficulties to contend with. Tensions are really high when our American friends visit, since we want to make sure the team is well taken care of. If anyone falls sick, we must take good care of her since they are always more sensitive to Kenyan conditions. We try hard to speak in English so we can communicate well, but often our American sisters speak too quickly for us, and use jargon we do not understand. That can be a strain on us. We know that they deal with climate differences, jet lag, and some food issues, so we try to be very careful with these things. And we are always fearful about the possible theft of their possessions; we make sure to host them in places that have good security, and we always contact the Chief of a given area so he can keep things secure.

I have told the United States team leaders how much there is to do before a team comes. Because all this preparation is done by Kenyan leaders, we have learned many new skills. Things that would have seemed impossible for us a few years ago are now part of our preparation before each team comes. Things like choosing a work site, determining materials needed and purchasing and delivering them, finding appropriate lodging and making deposits, planning a menu and training the women that we will work with. Our group members are trained in many areas. We remind them about good hygiene and cleanliness. We talk about good character and how to interact with team members. We also talk about self-control, which to us means having control of your desires and impulses. It would be easy to be envious of the western women's possessions, yet we teach our women to not ask for things and to treat the team as guests at all times. Those cooking the team meals are taught what is necessary for the team to not get sick, and the importance of using only clean water. All these areas are part of our transformation and help us grow as individuals and as an organization.

As you can imagine, this work exhausts us, yet we often have no time to recover. When we return to our homes, our normal, everyday workload is still waiting for us. Some will go straight to the fields. Others have other employment that has been neglected for two weeks. Many leaders must travel to visit the women in their groups (who were not a part of the work team experience) to encourage the work they are doing together. As leaders we are able to hold a Regional Program Managers meeting, where we thank God for the visit of the work team and pray for God to grant them journey mercies back home. We also review our strengths and weaknesses. Then we break for a week, without any meetings, to relax, stay with our families, and catch up on neglected work.

As much work as it is to host them, we still experience the presence of our work teams as a great blessing. They enlighten us and provide the fellowship of dancing, singing, and good communication. They work with us well—and don't discriminate at all! They are always caring and loving, and treat us as their sisters. They also help us understand the importance of helping one another, teaching our women's groups new ways to interact and share.

Boni: Of course, these visits are hard on the American visitors as well, but in different ways. But we remind everyone that the strains of working in a very different cultural context can lead to personal transformation; and that is a mindset that PFP desires to instill in our work team members. Often in the training prior to travel, when discussing the physical work that the team will do in Kenya, women become concerned that it may be too much for them: "I don't know if I can work in the sun for six hours!" The response is usually, "Could you sit in the shade and hear someone's story? That is more important than how much physical work you get done!" Sure enough, in the *post*-trip debrief sessions, team members will often emphasize that the most important aspects of their experience had everything to do with relationships. Our time in Kenya is about participating in relationship-building experiences that are life changing for Americans and

Kenyans alike. Building a base for a water tank will always get done one way or another, but the stories we hold in our hearts are what yields lasting mutual impact.

I recall one woman on our team, Linda, who said she was "changed forever" when she walked for water with several Kenyan women. While Linda is an athlete in great condition, carrying forty pounds of water up a hill in the heat was one of the hardest things she had ever done. She shared, "I did this just *once*. When I think of our Kenyan friends doing this every day, forever, I feel overwhelmed. I walked just a mile. Some of them walk five miles daily. It has changed my view of their world and mine as well!"

Karen was also on that same team. Before she met us in Nairobi, she had climbed Mount Kilimanjaro and ended up arriving in Kenya exhausted. On her first day with the PFP women, she was fatigued and discouraged. In her words, "Several team members came to my room to comfort me, but it didn't really help. Then Agnes came to my room with tenderness and warmth. She said she'd heard I didn't feel well and wanted to pray with me. She took my face in her hands and said, 'You are my sister, and you matter to me'. It was so authentic, and went deep into my soul. This changed the trip for me and actually changed my life! I think of this interaction daily."

Agnes: And of course, these short-term visits change a lot of Kenyan lives as well. During one of the visits, we were blessed to be taught in the afternoons by Dr. Alicia, a member of the PFP US team. She changed so many of our ideas about our health. Women asked many questions about giving birth and keeping our babies healthy. So many babies die soon after birth. One thing we learned was that it was good to give birth in a hospital. Most of our women distrust hospitals, but she explained the many ways a hospital can help us. We trusted her because she worked with us, laughed with us, and seemed to respect us. Now, two years later, many more women are getting medical help during their pregnancies and using hospitals when needed.

One of our women, Grace, is another example of transformation. The American team members who worked at Grace's house during their trip were eager to get to know her. They spent time hearing her story, sitting side by side, holding her hand, having tea together, and generally affirming her and her situation. You see, Grace suffered from fistula and had tried to keep it a secret. She had isolated herself because of the smell that accompanies this medical condition. She had not been to church in years and kept herself apart from other women. Yet she felt safe to share her story with the visiting team members in a way she hadn't before. Because of that conversation, she later inquired at the hospital to see if anything could be done for her condition. The women of PFP Kenya encouraged her, supported her through her appointments, and helped pay for the surgery. A huge transformation took place. Grace went on to marry her partner in a church wedding, and PFP friends put on the reception. Now she meets with friends and has become an active member of her PFP group. Grace was able to put aside her shame and allow herself to be affirmed, encouraged, and empowered to make life changes. This huge change happened as a result of being heard without judgment.

Boni: One of the Kenyan Program Managers, Sue, believes that having a work team visit is very exciting for everyone. While it is a lot of work to prepare for a team visit, she believes it is worth it. Women's group members feel honored to be with the team. In her opinion, they make new friends, sometimes see people they have met before, learn a lot from each other, and get new ideas for improving their projects. They dance, sing, share, laugh, and pray together. With the 2020 work team, Americans shared themselves at a level that was unusual to Kenyans. Before long Kenyans were sharing their stories in the same way. They told us it was wonderful to hear deep sharing, and new ways of sharing opened for them also.

Agnes: By the time the Americans leave for home and the Kenyans return to their daily routines, most of us feel that we have more in common with these sisters than we could have imagined. We are more alike than not. We are truly sisters in Christ, and that is what defines us. Our skin color, our economic differences, our country's values—are not the things that really matter. We all want what is best for our families. We all would do anything to protect our children, and we want our families to thrive. We all long to know God more intimately and to understand what God wants of us. We all want to be safe and have some level of security. We all want a future filled with hope. It is a wonderful feeling to talk with our American sisters about these desires that we share in common.

When they visit, it is a gift to us that the American women surrender their needs to us. We have learned so much by providing fully for them. And perhaps more importantly, trust is built between us.

Boni: This is the work we've come to understand as the most important work of our short-term visits—the work of cultivating authentic relationships. It is always our common prayer that as we work together in Kenya, we will be able to maintain our commitment to Jesus and to what we believe he asks of us.

Agnes: I always emphasize to Kenyan women that we must remain open and willing to share our true thoughts and feelings in the experience of working together, and to be bold and honest about our hopes for transformation.

Boni: And I emphasize to American women that there is never a time to presume that we know more than Kenyans do about their circumstances— and that we as Americans must always be on guard against presumptions of superiority.

Only by continuing to foster such mutual openness and trust can we continue together the good work that the Lord began. May God give us strength for the work ahead.

Agnes Kioko

Agnes is an accomplished, optimistic leader. She works closely with women and girls to help in poverty eradication. Through her work at Path from Poverty, Agnes has seen first-hand that empowering women and girls can bring transformational improvement in the health and prosperity of families, communities and societies. Agnes believes in team effectiveness, realism and humanism. She is always goal-oriented. Agnes lives in Kenya with her husband together with her two children.

Boni Piper

Boni is the President of the board of Directors of Path from Poverty, a Christian non-profit based in Seattle and presently working in Kenya. She has degrees from Geneva College, Seattle Pacific University, and Reformed Presbyterian Seminary where she completed a year-long Mission Training course. Boni believes that mutuality, coathority, and deep respect for each other is crucial for effective, life-giving transformation. The beautiful results are the deep friendships and mutual empowerment.

16

Short-Term Missions and Disaster Relief

Chris Sheach

On August 14, 2021, as an earthquake rocked the island nation of Haiti, I was reminded of the *first* time I arrived in Haiti, after the 2010 earthquake which devastated the country. I worked for an international humanitarian aid agency with a multimillion dollar rebuilding project and found myself flying in with a plane full of "spring break" missionaries. Growing up as a Third Culture Kid myself, I had seen all kinds of short-term mission trips on the receiving end.[1] For a time I was in support of them, believing that mono-culture Christians would grow in their faith through their exposure to other cultures. And the short trips to orphanages and schools seemed to do little harm.

Later though, in my career as a professional disaster relief manager, I came to understand that in many post-disaster contexts, even well-meaning short-term teams could actually cause a good deal of harm. Too often (as was the case with the 2010 earthquake in Haiti) I had to work with such teams—and it made no sense to me that untrained, unequipped volunteers would take up time, space, and resources that could be used for saving lives.

1. TCKs are raised in a culture other than their parents's or their passport culture during a significant part of their childhood. See Van Reken, et al. *Third Culture Kids.*

As part of my relief work, I have been trained to minimize my impact on affected communities. Once I hit the ground in the wake of a disaster, I provide my own shelter, medical care, food, and water for weeks or months at a time. I am prepared to stay in unsanitary or even hostile environments, without relying on guides, translators or chauffeurs. In contrast, the many teams of young people that poured into Haiti in 2010 took up space in the few earthquake-resistant shelters that were available. Their buses filled the roads and impeded the process of clearing rubble. Their need for American foods meant that local stores stocked Diet Coke, strawberry jam and imported bread in place of essentials like rice and beans.

Of course, there were teams visiting Haiti long before the 2010 earthquake. Yet the international attention brought on by the disaster made Haiti a target context, and every weekend flight for several years after the quake had a short-term mission team on board. I intentionally flew mid-week to avoid conversations with these groups; I am sure they didn't want to hear my thoughts about their "Montana Loves Haiti" t-shirts, and I most certainly did not want to hear their stories of self-discovery.

Since that time, while I still believe that short-term teams are usually not an effective response to disasters, I have also come to believe that *in some cases, with the right people and the right preparation,* there is a place for short-term teams in disaster relief. In this essay I will point out the challenges that make the STM approach less effective at relief work; yet I will also describe my involvement with two teams that opened me up to possibilities—teams that had actually found a way to do more good than harm in a disaster relief setting. Through them, I came to understand how and why STMs *can potentially* add value in a disaster response situation.

Deep Understanding

Short-term team responses to disasters are typically ineffective because there is simply not enough time to gain an understanding of the context of need. Naturally, when churches and Christian organizations see the severity of needs caused by a disaster, they feel the compassionate impulse to send help. Unfortunately, while reconstruction, food, and medical supplies seem "easy" needs to meet, sending organizations usually have no sense of how to engage the deeper systemic issues: the deep-rooted social, political, cultural and economic systemic failures which are the underlying causes for unmet needs. A disaster can be defined as "a serious disruption of the functioning of a society, causing widespread human, material, or environmental losses which exceed the ability of the affected society to cope using its own resources."[2] When more than one thousand agencies of all types responded to the 2010 earthquake in Haiti (many engaging in international response for the first time), their overwhelming presence exacerbated the fragility of the infrastructure and networks that were actually working to sustain the response, and their impact slowed recovery immensely.

Well-meaning short-term responders can also unknowingly impact the economic systems even as they offer aid to those in need. After a disaster, supply chains are often bottlenecked because of damaged infrastructure like airports, seaports, and bridges. The resultant national food shortages can be exacerbated when visiting foreigners buy what food is available in local shops; in some cases, they might be unknowingly taking it from the mouths of the most vulnerable. Similarly, when teams of foreigners (who are used to a high minimum standard of comfort) use already-scarce fuel to run generators for electricity after dark or to heat water for hot showers, it can mean that the local people cannot get enough fuel even to cook their dinners. Any short-term team that wants to avoid becoming part of the problem must figure out in advance how to be self-sufficient and not dependent on local resources.

Disasters tend to destabilize governments and can lead to extreme rates of crime and insecurity; the presence of foreigners (who usually don't have the necessary understanding of these dynamics) can easily complicate such a situation and make it worse for everyone. After the 2010 earthquake, one of my Haitian colleagues was carjacked by bandits. I remember waiting days for a government document, because the man who needed to sign it had been kidnapped and his family was trying to pay the ransom. At another time, our warehouse was robbed at gunpoint by gang members who were considered "untouchable" by police. Working effectively in this sort of context takes training and cultural savvy. Because short-term teams don't know (and don't have time to learn) the ground rules for staying safe, and because they represent relative wealth, they are easy (and more lucrative) targets for crime. Their presence often invites great risk to themselves, and also to those hosting them in the communities they intend to serve.

2. International Strategy for Disaster Reduction, *Disaster Risk Reduction*, 9.

Relevant Skills and Necessary Character

In light of these challenges, it is easy to understand why a typical American youth group should avoid trying to serve in a disaster relief situation. A wiser approach would be to send people more established in their careers, with a clearly relevant skills to offer and—ideally—some experience of hardship. Doctors, nurses, engineers, and skilled builders for example have greater potential for providing effective aid. Disaster settings are, in fact, a great place for short rotational teams of professionals to serve; organizations such as Medical Teams International (MTI) and Doctors Without Borders (MSF) have perfected this approach.

Still, skills are no substitute for thorough, nuanced learning about a given context. And skills are of little use when practitioners do not have the necessary character traits to serve in relief contexts—traits like perseverance, courage, and grace. I have met trauma surgeons and ER nurses who were completely overwhelmed by having to work under a tent in high heat with no electricity. I've dealt with engineers who rejected all locally available building materials as inferior, and insisted on importing expensive materials that made sense only according to the building codes of their home country. The reason that MTI and MSF manage to create high impact, sustainable teams has to do with their personnel screening processes, and the very rigorous orientations they require for their volunteers. Any sending organization should practice such rigorous standards when considering the sort of people they should be sending into a disaster relief situation.

The Right Kind of Team with the Right Kind of People

In 2012, I hosted a team of volunteers from Engineering Ministries International (EMI) in Haiti. The mission was focused on providing analysis and recommendations to local engineers on designs for preventing and mitigating flooding and erosion. The team surveyed the area, and *only after taking the time to ask questions and to listen attentively* to the wisdom of the local people did they write up a list of recommendations. Most importantly, the recommendations they offered were varied, and presented with clear estimations of cost, complexity, and maintenance requirements. This team brought obvious value with their presence: their wealth of current knowledge in their fields provided fresh perspectives for their Haitian peers, and their recommendations presented multiple possible options. Importantly though, their expertise was balanced with the humble acknowledgement that there was much they did not know about the local context; in a truly copowering dynamic, they trusted themselves to the contextual expertise of their local colleagues. By leaving the decision about the best way forward in the hands of the local engineers and their communities, the EMI team communicated mutual respect and humility.

EMI has sent many short-term teams around the world, and the organization understands the importance of copowerment in ministry. Because of the difficult working context in Haiti, even years after the earthquake, they were very careful to choose a team of qualified engineers who were also prepared for the frustrations and discomforts they would face. Every member of this team except one had gained experience and wisdom on previous STM trips; yet even the first-timer had served with the military in Afghanistan, so she too was familiar with hardship assignments.

Frankly, if STMs are to serve effectively in disaster relief settings, they really do need to be prepared for the worst. And that means that most schools, churches, and sending agencies should not be sending teams into such settings. I have worked in disaster scenes where there was no running water for months—and no toilets, showers, and of course no washing machines. In Port-au-Prince after the 2010 earthquake, the smell of rotting human flesh, raw sewage, and burning tires was suffocating, and the toxic soot seemed to infiltrate every pore of my skin. Months later, we would still be finding bodies in the rubble of collapsed buildings—and sometimes, even the rumble of a passing truck caused people to dive for cover in terror. Disasters are inherently traumatic for those affected, but can also be very traumatic for those who take part in response and recovery.

The Global Church in Relief and Development

CHAD ISENHART

IT MAY BE STRANGE to think about disaster relief as compatible with STM. However, in my position as the Director of Foursquare

Disaster Relief, I have come across many experiences where short-term trips can be used to connect with the global church and assist them through a crisis. However, there are a few important components to consider: the necessity of an invitation, understanding the importance of context, and the need for listening.

This dynamic was demonstrated on a recent short-term trip that our team made to Puerto Rico, to teach church leaders and laity about spiritual and emotional care for people impacted by disasters. Puerto Rico had experienced a series of natural disasters and severe economic challenges over a period of four to five years. With so many people impacted from their congregations, pastors were looking for ways to help people navigate the emotional journey through these disasters, in addition to offering prayer and encouragement through Scripture. It is important to note that we went in response to a request made by the national Foursquare Church in Puerto Rico. Our goal is always to minimize the time spent in the relief context by cultural outsiders—and to eventually hand over the continued relief to local leadership. Until that transition can happen, even our short-term workers serve under the guidance of national leaders, who know their own cultures, people, languages, and traditions best.

As Americans, it would have been natural for us to make our own decisions in advance about what kind of training Puerto Ricans needed. However, our team had been armed with the understanding that, because we were not Puerto Rican, our systems and our culture were likely to yield assumptions that were out of sync with the realities of the context. We began instead by engaging in conversations with leaders in the Puerto Rico Foursquare church, including several culture brokers—individuals who had formed relationships in both cultures, gained insight from lived experience in both contexts, and earned the respect of both parties. We spent time becoming aware of the needs at hand, and listening to what our Puerto Rican colleagues were envisioning in response to the needs. Too often representatives of western churches, in their compassionate zeal to respond to urgent needs, skip this important step. Historically, we westerners have been quick to jump in, bringing whatever it is *we* think is needed—without asking if what we are bringing is truly helpful in that particular context.

During this stage of our efforts in Puerto Rico, we prioritized the importance of listening—and in doing so came to understand exactly what sort of relief was needed. Importantly, our Puerto Rican hosts explained that the needs of their communities went beyond material supplies only; these leaders also wanted to be able to address the deep emotional impact that recent disasters were having on people's souls. In response, we were able to present spiritual and emotional care principles to build a foundation of support and healing for their congregations. Granted, our training team represented decades of experience that qualified them to teach on this topic. However, we always try to remember that expertise does not guarantee effectiveness from context to context. The content of the training sessions, and even the ways in which the sessions were taught, needed the shaping influence of our Puerto Rican coworkers. In this copowerment dynamic, both Puerto Ricans and Americans were made more effective, and in the process developed closer relationships—as co-laborers and friends. Through experiences like this, we continue to learn just what it means to see ourselves as merely a part of the collective mission of the global church.

Chad Isenhart

Chad Isenhart lives in Tacoma, Washington, and is the Director of Foursquare Disaster Relief on behalf of The Foursquare Church based out of Los Angeles, California. He has worked in humanitarian relief and development for over twelve years and has a master's in International Humanitarian Affairs from the University of York in York, England. Chad has been married for nine years to his wife Jordyn, and has three beautiful busy children. Chad lives at the intersection of Matthew 28 and James 1:27, and finds it his joy to help churches around the world find ways to love their communities in ways they may never have thought possible.

A Good Team Overcomes Failed Planning

I had yet another opportunity to work with a team that showed me new possibilities for STMs in disaster relief. Again, this took place in Haiti, just after Hurricane Matthew ripped the roofs off houses across the south of the country in 2016. During the Hurricane Matthew recovery, I was asked to host a team from an American donor church to help with house repairs. In this particular project, funding was low—so we focused on training families how to make temporary repairs with tarps, rope and salvaged materials until more support could be raised for permanent fixes. Unfortunately, something got lost in the communication process, and the American team arrived fully expecting to be swinging hammers and engaging in rebuilding and permanent repairs. With no materials for that, they ended up spending time every day visiting damaged homes, helping where they could by offering advice on tying better knots or resecuring a loose tarp. In short, there was not enough real work for them to do—a complete failure of mission design on my part! When the team returned from the field and recounted their stories during a debrief, I asked them what they had learned. One team member said that, in not being able to feel really useful, she had been forced to slow down and to begin to *really see* the families they were visiting. Another person explained that, because of the less driven and goal-centered mode they were in, they discovered opportunities to pray for the Haitians who had lost so much. She explained:

> I saw an older lady sit down after cleaning up the ruins of her house, and I just wanted to pray for her. So I asked one of the Haitian team to translate, and asked if I could pray with her. She looked surprised and then said, "Oh, yes." After that we just started asking everyone if we could pray with them.

After that American team had left, I asked the Haitian relief team what they had thought about the trip. In addition to telling me how I could have planned it a lot better (which was definitely true), they told me that their interactions with the team had been spiritually uplifting for them. "We're so busy trying to fix homes, that we had never thought to just pray with the families in those homes. It felt good to bring Jesus to work with us," they explained. After discussing this further, they suggested putting together a future staff retreat to which they would invite their new American friends to help lead them a time of worship and reflection. Through their interactions with the visiting team, the Haitians had realized that the tyranny of the urgent had overtaken their work of ministry; they had needed someone from outside to help them see that.

Short-Term Missions and Disaster Relief

I am not suggesting that the role of STM in disasters should be focused on door-to-door prayer. In certain contexts, that would be highly dangerous, illegal, or inappropriate. I also do not believe it should be limited to technical experts. My purpose in recounting these stories is to highlight key elements I see for fruitful STM in disaster recovery, which I learned from these experiences:

1. Being flexible: Recognizing that the mission had changed, the second team looked for opportunity. In disaster response, the situation changes daily, plans get canceled, and yet we must continue to provide the best aid possible. Teams that understand the transient nature of the work will be more fruitful.

2. Giving what you have: For the engineering team, what they had was not a *better* way, but a *different* way. They gave their suggestions to their peers—the local engineers—and let the local experts work with the communities to identify what was best for their context. Also, it is important that teams recognize that their spiritual gifts—not just hard skills—are being called on during mission trips. In the case of the second team described above, Haitian communities did not really need their physical help of the second team, who had no real skills in making and repairing shanties. Nevertheless, the communities were blessed by the support, encouragement and prayer of fellow believers.

3. Serving the local workers: I honestly believe that both teams were more of a blessing to the team of Haitian disaster relief workers than to the local community, as "co-workers in God's service."[3] When I took a management role in disaster relief services, I learned that my job was not to minister to disaster-impacted communities directly. Rather, my work was to support the local teams on the front lines of disaster relief, through resourcing and encouraging them. Disaster relief is a spiritually taxing job. Many responders work dusk to dawn for fourteen days straight or more. There is little time for religious

3. 1 Cor 3:9 (NIV).

services or communal fellowship. I would love to see more STMs support the spiritual wellbeing of humanitarian aid workers, both local and international.

After a decade of cynicism, these Haitian experiences have helped me turn the page. Under the right conditions, with the right people and the right sort of preparation, I've come to believe that there is space for STM in a post-disaster setting. These teams need to be prepared for very tough conditions and inevitable changes in a very uncertain context. And while there is definitely a role for technical or professional teams, even they must be prepared for an environment which severely limits the practices of their skills. Importantly, STM teams must be prepared to offer spiritual support even as they seek to meet physical needs. And finally, more than anything, foreign teams need the humility and grace to serve as *coworkers* with their sisters and brothers already present in the local community.

Chris Sheach

Chris Sheach has over fifteen years of experience in disaster management, organizational leadership and humanitarian response. He has led disaster response operations for international Christian NGOs on four continents, including hurricanes, earthquakes and tsunami, as well as in conflict zones. During his career, Chris has developed networks on every continent and specializes in multiagency coordinated relief and recovery programs. Along the way he has learned seven languages and picked up a love of soccer, exotic food, and strong coffee. Currently Chris is an Instructor of Emergency Management at Arkansas Tech University and a volunteer firefighter. Now that he travels less, he has time to serve as a Governing Member of the Association of Professionals in Humanitarian Assistance and Protection and as a member of the board of the Disaster Accountability Project

Bibliography

International Strategy for Disaster Reduction, *UNISDR on Disaster Risk Reduction,* 2009.

17

Re-Imagining STM
Copowerment for a Global Church

Cyrus Mad-Bondo, *with* Casey Duthier

For good reasons, the prevalent practices of short-term missions these days are being critically evaluated. Increasingly, scholars and practitioners are calling for new modes and models to displace dysfunctional ones, while some are recommending that we jettison STM altogether. I would argue that, while our thinking about short-term trips does indeed need a major overhaul, we ought not to give up on STMs entirely. Rather, we must learn from best practices even as we design and implement new STM alternatives.

However, I would suggest that there is no way forward that is not grounded in mutually respectful collaboration between stakeholder churches. Churches in every part of the world must confront historical power imbalances, racial biases, and economic disparities, and discover ways to relate interculturally as coequal members of one global church. Others in this volume argue (rightly) for reimagined STM practices that are grounded in authentic, long-term relationships between churches in different parts of the world. If indeed relationships are the future of short-term missions, the fundamental question we must ask is: how do we actually make those intercultural connections, and cultivate partnerships with communities of like heart and mind? I suggest here some critical practices for initiating and maintaining authentic, intercultural, interchurch relationships including careful *vetting*, practicing *copowerment*, and establishing *long-term commitments*.

I must first confess my bias in favor of reforming STM practices rather than rejecting them out of hand. You see, I was on the "receiving end" of missionary efforts, as a child growing up in the Central African Republic. From the examples set by the missionaries who introduced the gospel to my family, I learned and internalized principles and practices of missions done effectively and well. As part of the third generation of believers in my family, I now serve as a leader at McLean Bible Church in Virginia, where it is my responsibility to help our church members live out the great commission, both locally and globally. In 2018, our ten thousand member church sent out nearly five hundred short-term missionaries on thirty-one mission trips. I facilitate short-term missions teams and encourage those who come back from these trips to live out the difference God has made in their hearts, either in their own communities or through mid-term and long-term missions work. This is all to say: while I understand all that is wrong with short-term missions, I've made it my life's work to pay attention to what is right about them, and also to advocate for reformation grounded in principles of coequal, long-term relationship.

Careful Vetting

Too often, cross-cultural STM connections are initiated in ways that work against the development of a healthy partnership. Often, leaders of a sending church will begin with their own agenda, based on such factors as media hype surrounding the current social problem of the day, the ministry interests of the most vocal congregants, or even scheduling convenience. If we decide though to think in authentic relationship terms, our process has to be more intentional and discerning. My advice to any community or organization wanting to engage short-term missions is to take the time to learn as much as possible—not just about potential ministry partners, but also about the strengths and needs they would bring to the relationship.

In essence, we need to engage in a process of vetting potential partner churches, and to have the humility to allow those churches to vet us as well.

It must be acknowledged that this vetting process isn't easy, since it often involves political, cultural, and even language barriers. Yet even though it takes time to build relationships and truly get to know potential partner communities, it is always wise to invest in this research process before making commitments to partnerships. In many cases, this process can be helped by a cultural liaison or a cultural broker—someone who understands the contexts of both churches and is able to facilitate communication between them as they conceive of plans that are mutually understood and mutually beneficial.

In addition to my role at McLean Bible Church, I also work for an organization called World Help—a nonprofit that meets the needs of impoverished communities around the world. In both roles, I connect churches and ministries: as a matchmaker of sorts, I help potential partners do careful assessment of factors including characteristic interests, organizational history, resources, needs, and areas of potential reciprocal influence. I work to ensure that both hosts and senders of short-term workers are somehow made better by the work they do together. I believe it is an act of humility on the part of those who see themselves as "sending" churches (particularly in America) to acknowledge that they need support in this vetting and connecting process. Churches and ministries who are willing to listen, take the time to consult with cultural insiders, and invite the perspective of those who have committed their lives to building cross-cultural ministry partnerships will have the best chance of success in building a good collaborative relationship that lasts.

As an important part of the vetting process, I recommend starting with an exploratory trip. The exploratory trip is a key first step in understanding the impact of the host organization and to begin vision casting for the potential partnership. It is an opportunity for the sending church to familiarize itself with the local culture and begin to recognize the wisdom and the voices of local leaders. In this process, the visiting church humbly acknowledges that there is much to be learned from their hosts and seeks to learn from their insider perspective.

At the same time, the host community must seek to learn as much as possible about their visitors and the community they represent. This is not always easy, since in contexts (such as Africa) the culture conditions people to be deferential to foreigners, and to avoid evaluative or personal questioning that could be perceived as intrusive or challenging. In part, these relational patterns grew out of a history of colonialism, and are continued in the unequal donor-client dynamics fostered by foreign NGOs. Yet if a relationship is to be established on the grounds of mutual respect and coequal status, both of the potential partners must resist (and encourage each other to resist) these socially-prescribed roles. In treating one another as equal members of the body of Christ, we honor God and bear witness to God's love that unites us in common purpose.

Practicing Copowerment

Churches involved in short-term missions must be willing to engage in a contextualized way, one that is open to transformation and empowerment on both sides. In other words, they should seek to establish a relationship of copowerment, "*a dynamic of mutual exchange through which both sides of a social equation are made stronger and more effective by the other.*"[1] This requires that both sides of the STM relationship be bold to give out of their strengths and resources, and humble to acknowledge the places of need that might be met by the other.

A great example of this dynamic can be found in the story of my family's faith journey, and the missionaries who invested in it. My parents experienced salvation through the work of missionaries in my home country, the Central African Republic. The missionaries taught my community the gospel message—but they also left space for us to interpret and apply the Word in ways that were relevant to our place and our people—and were therefore more effectively life-changing. At the same time, the missionaries sought to learn from the community, so that they could do their work more effectively—but also that they might better understand the gospel in the new light of a different cultural perspective. These are the contextualized, mutually-transformative, copowering dynamics that characterize healthy STM relationships.

Often though, STMs are one-sided, and focused on the needs to be met in the host context. At the other end of the spectrum, some STM teams are focused solely on their own personal development—to the detriment of their work of service.[2] When we think instead in terms of *mutual* transformation, parties on both sides of the relationship must be open and responsive to God's movement in their lives. As I learned from my father, it is important not only to ask "What you are going to do with your education?"—but also to ask "What has your education done to you?" The STM experience should change participants in some way. In most cases, the main focus of a trip really should be service that meets needs in a host

---

1. See Dr. Inslee's observations in the introduction of this volume, xvii–xxiv.
2. See Jay Matenga's observations in chapter 3 of this volume, 32–38.

context. Yet such a trip can and should also be framed as an educational experience—one that teaches us about another way of life and a new culture, but also makes us more aware of God's work—and even helps us to better understand God.

In a healthy, copowering STM relationship, one of the goals must be transformation on both sides of the equation; and for that reason, the objectives of a trip should be negotiated and defined in advance by both sides, working together. In this "negotiation" we do need to be careful not to relate to one another in transactional terms. In other words, good STM interactions are less like the *quid pro quo* exchanges of business, and more like the easy give and take of an affectionate friendship. Our motivating question must never become, "How can we make sure each side is getting what they want?" Instead, we ought to think in copowerment terms and ask, "How can we be better together?" In that sense we establish *the development of the relationship itself* as one of the key objectives of STM visits, and that in itself is a worthy goal.

Long-term Relationships

It might seem like a contradiction at first, to think of developing *long-term* intercultural relationships based in *short-term* missions. I argue though that this is the best way to do both. As in any good friendship, an intercultural relationship between faith communities depends on the belief that we are in the relationship for the long-haul. When we trust that our friends will stick with us, even (and especially) in lean and difficult times, then the relationship is allowed to deepen over time.

At McLean Bible Church, once we have taken the time to establish a partnership with another church or ministry overseas, we see our regular visits as essential to growing that relationship over time. Each time we visit with a short-term team, our partner ministry is able to show us expansions of their initiatives; when those projects arose out of collaborations with our church, our in-person visits allow us the opportunity to celebrate together, to affirm our working partnership, and on those grounds begin to envision future projects together.

It is always better to cultivate relationships that grow deeper and stronger over time—as opposed to one-off interactions that go an inch deep and a mile wide. Sure, there might be instant gratification—and great photo ops—when a short-term team spends a week handing out bags of rice or playing soccer with kids at an orphanage. Yet there is greater joy in seeing God growing a partner church over the course of years . . . or in tracking the long-term economic impact of a grassroots development organization we helped to establish together. And we as a sending church grow along with our partner ministries—learning principles and best practices with each new collaborative project, and glean wisdom even when some of our joint projects fail. The key practice that makes any of this possible, of course, is our overt commitment—to the relationship and to the shared work—for the long-term.

Implications for Re-imagining Short-term Missions

When it comes to current STM practices, we are in a season of crisis and opportunity—and that is a good thing. We must devote ourselves to the task of re-evaluating just what it is we've been doing in the name of "mission." I wonder though if we might approach this challenge from a different angle. What if "short-term missions done better" was not an end in itself? What if we made it instead a means to a greater end? In this globalized world we live in, the possibilities for creating intercultural, interchurch relationships seem endless. In this interconnected age, when churches and ministries can easily establish long-term, copowering connections from wherever they are in the world, the prospect of a truly global church now seems utterly feasible. What if we began to look at short-term mission trips as a means to make the church more relationally global? If that were to happen, then perhaps the real question we ought to be asking is, should we be calling them "short-term missions" at all?

Cyrus Mad-Bondo

Cyrus is the Global Outreach Mobilization Leader for Mclean Bible Church. In his role, he leads the Global Outreach by equipping, sending and caring well for all MBC's missionaries. Cyrus has served for twelve years at World Help (a Christian organization), strengthening national ministries and leading mission trips as Vice President and Africa Chief Strategist. He is originally from the Central African Republic, where he met Julie, his wife of thirty-two years. He and Julie have two adult children, and two grandsons. Cyrus received a bachelor's degree at Malone University and his master's degree at Liberty University. He has traveled and shared the gospel across Africa, Central America, Central and Southeast Asia

Casey Duthiers

Casey Duthiers is an independent contractor supporting nonprofits through project management, marketing, and fundraising. She is a PhD candidate at Biola University's Cook School of Intercultural Studies. She lives in Atlanta, GA.

Discussion Questions

THE FOLLOWING QUESTIONS ARE meant to create "conversation" between this section's themes and your own perspectives and experiences. They are intended to be useful for both sides of the STM relationship: guests who travel to serve other communities, and the hosts who receive them. While these questions offer thought-provoking prompts for journaling, meditation, and prayer, they also serve as starting places for group discussion with others in your community who care about reimagining STM. We highly recommend both modes of engagement when that is possible.

1. This book presents some new ways to think about and practice STM. If you believe that much of what we call STM is broken, dysfunctional, and theologically-suspect, what stops you and your community from creating alternatives to the status quo? For sending communities, what holds people back from designing and experimenting with new ways to engage the needs of the world? For those who host STM teams, what holds you back from creating and implementing better ways to collaborate interculturally with other communities in the global church?

2. In the essay "Re-Imagining STM: Copowerment for a Global Church," the authors emphasize the importance of copowerment as a key dynamic in developing and maintaining good relationships between partner churches. If you and your community were to start thinking more like coequal members of the global church, what might be some

first steps you could take toward building copowering relationships with churches in other parts of the world?

3. Agnes Kioko and Boni Piper tell the story of a close and lasting friendship—and of the very relational model of cross-cultural engagement that made it possible. Can you imagine the development of such authentic friendships happening in the context of STMs as you have experienced them? In your opinion, is this even a necessary or reasonable objective to shoot for in the process of reimagining short-term missions?

4. How do you respond to Craig Greenfield, Cyrus Mad-Bono, and others in this book who suggest that we need to stop using the term "short-term missions?"

Concluding Questions

1. Take some time to list and perhaps journal about three to five learning points that have stuck with you as you've been reading this book.

2. When you consider these take-aways, how do they make you feel? Are you hopeful? Discouraged? Excited? Remorseful? Whatever your feelings, take time to write them down, and in the process ask yourself: why do I feel this way?

3. If any of the authors in this book have inspired you to action, what are some practical next steps you could take toward re-imagining short-term missions? If you are not already in conversation about these things with others in your community, how might you invite them? If you have working relationships with communities in other parts of the world, what would make it possible to collaborate with them—both to evaluate past STM practices, and to dream of better ways to do good and glorify God together?